D1240342

## LOT VIEWING
**Waldorf Astoria • Sutton Suite**
301 Park Avenue
New York, New York 10022

Saturday, January 2, 2010 • 9:00 AM - 7:00 PM ET
Sunday, January 3, 2010 • 8:00 AM - 6:00 PM ET
Monday, January 4, 2010 • 8:00 AM - 6:00 PM ET
Tuesday, January 5, 2010 • 8:00 AM - 4:00 PM ET

*View Lots Online at HA.com/WorldCoin*

## LIVE FLOOR BIDDING
Bid in person during the floor sessions.

## LIVE TELEPHONE BIDDING *(floor sessions only)*
Phone bidding must be arranged on or before
Thursday, December 31, 2009, by 12:00 PM CT.
Client Service: 866-835-3243.

## HERITAGE Live!™ BIDDING
*Bid live* from your location, anywhere in the world,
during the Auction using our HERITAGE Live!™ program
at HA.com/Live

## INTERNET BIDDING
Internet absentee bidding ends at 10:00 PM CT
the evening before each session. HA.com/WorldCoin

## FAX BIDDING
Fax bids must be received on or before Thursday,
December 31, 2009, by 12:00 PM CT. Fax: 214-409-1425

## MAIL BIDDING
Mail bids must be received on or before
Thursday, December 31, 2009.

*Please see "Choose Your Bidding Method" in the back of this
catalog for specific details about each of these bidding methods.*

## LIVE AUCTION
**SIGNATURE® FLOOR SESSIONS 1-3**
*(Floor, Telephone, HERITAGE Live!,™ Internet, Fax, and Mail)*
**Waldorf Astoria • Norse Suite**
301 Park Avenue • New York, New York 10022

### SESSION 1
Sunday, January 3, 2010 • 4:00 PM ET • Lots 20001-21201
Featuring The Canadiana Collection • Lots 20001–20365
For Lots 20366 - 21201, see separate catalog

### SESSION 2 *(see separate catalog)*
Monday, January 4, 2010 • 1:00 PM ET • Lots 21202–22098

### SESSION 3 *(see separate catalog)*
Monday, January 4, 2010 • 6:00 PM ET • Lots 22099–23044

## NON FLOOR/NON PHONE BIDDING SESSION 4
*(HERITAGE Live!,™ Internet, Fax, and Mail only)*

### SESSION 4 *(see separate catalog)*
Tuesday, January 12, 2010 • 12:00 PM CT • Lots 25001–27087

## AUCTION RESULTS
Immediately available at HA.com/WorldCoin

## LOT SETTLEMENT AND PICK-UP
Monday, January 4 • 10:00 AM - 1:00 PM ET
Tuesday, January 5 • 9:00 AM - 12:00 PM ET

*Extended Payment Terms available. See details in the back of this catalog.*

*Lots are sold at an approximate rate of 200 lots per hour, but it
is not uncommon to sell 150 lots or 300 lots in any given hour.*

*This auction is subject to a 15% Buyer's Premium.*

---

THIS AUCTION IS PRESENTED AND CATALOGED BY HERITAGE NUMISMATIC AUCTIONS, INC.

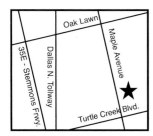

Heritage World Headquarters

# HERITAGE HA.com
## Auction Galleries

Home Office • 3500 Maple Avenue, 17th Floor • Dallas, Texas 75219
Design District Annex • 1518 Slocum Street • Dallas, Texas 75207
214.528.3500 | 800.872.6467 | 214.409.1425 (fax)
Direct Client Service Line: Toll Free 1.866.835.3243 • Email: Bid@HA.com

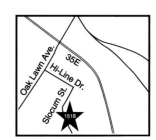

Heritage Design District Annex

# DIRECTORY FOR DEPARTMENT SPECIALISTS AND SERVICES

## COINS & CURRENCY

### COINS – UNITED STATES
HA.com/Coins

**Leo Frese**, Ext. 1294
Leo@HA.com
**David Mayfield**, Ext. 1277
DavidM@HA.com
**Jessica Aylmer**, Ext. 1706
JessicaA@HA.com
**Diedre Buchmoyer**, Ext. 1794
DiedreB@HA.com
**Win Callender**, Ext. 1415
WinC@HA.com
**Bert DeLaGarza**, Ext. 1795
BertD@HA.com
**Chris Dykstra**, Ext. 1380
ChrisD@HA.com
**Sam Foose**, Ext. 1227
SamF@HA.com
**Jason Friedman**, Ext. 1582
JasonF@HA.com
**Shaunda Fry**, Ext. 1159
ShaundaF@HA.com
**Jim Jelinski**, Ext. 1257
JimJ@HA.com
**Katherine Kurachek**, Ext. 1389
KK@HA.com
**Bob Marino**, Ext. 1374
BobMarino@HA.com
**Mike Sadler**, Ext. 1332
MikeS@HA.com

### RARE CURRENCY
HA.com/Currency

**Len Glazer**, Ext. 1390
Len@HA.com
**Allen Mincho**, Ext. 1327
Allen@HA.com
**Dustin Johnston**, Ext. 1302
Dustin@HA.com
**Michael Moczalla**, Ext. 1481
MichaelM@HA.com
**Jason Friedman**, Ext. 1582
JasonF@HA.com

### U.S. COINS PRIVATE TREATY SALES
HA.com/Coins

**Todd Imhof**, Ext. 1313
Todd@HA.com

### U.S. COINS PURCHASED
HA.com/Coins

**Jim Stoutjesdyk**, Ext. 1310
JimS@HA.com

### WORLD & ANCIENT COINS
HA.com/WorldCoins

**Warren Tucker**, Ext. 1287
WTucker@HA.com
**Cristiano Bierrenbach**, Ext. 1661
CrisB@HA.com
**Scott Cordry**, Ext. 1369
ScottC@HA.com

## COMICS & COMIC ART
HA.com/Comics

**Ed Jaster**, Ext. 1288
EdJ@HA.com
**Lon Allen**, Ext. 1261
LonA@HA.com
**Barry Sandoval**, Ext. 1377
BarryS@HA.com
**Todd Hignite**, Ext. 1790
ToddH@HA.com

## FINE ART

### AMERICAN & EUROPEAN PAINTINGS & SCULPTURE
HA.com/FineArt

**Edmund P. Pillsbury, Ph.D.**, Ext. 1533
EPP@HA.com
**Ed Jaster**, Ext. 1288
EdJ@HA.com
**Courtney Case**, Ext. 1293
CourtneyC@HA.com
**Marianne Berardi, Ph.D.**, Ext. 1506
MarianneB@HA.com
**Ariana Hartsock**, Ext. 1283
ArianaH@HA.com

### ART OF THE AMERICAN WEST
HA.com/WesternArt

**Michael Duty**, Ext. 1712
MichaelD@HA.com

### FURNITURE & DECORATIVE ART
HA.com/Decorative

**Tim Rigdon**, Ext. 1119
TimR@HA.com
**Meredith Meuwly**, Ext. 1631
MeredithM@HA.com
**Nicholas Dawes**, Ext. 1605
NickD@HA.com

### ILLUSTRATION ART
HA.com/Illustration

**Ed Jaster**, Ext. 1288
EdJ@HA.com
**Todd Hignite**, Ext. 1790
ToddH@HA.com

### MODERN & CONTEMPORARY ART
HA.com/Modern

**Frank Hettig**, Ext. 1157
FrankH@HA.com

### SILVER & VERTU
HA.com/Silver

**Tim Rigdon**, Ext. 1119
TimR@HA.com

### TEXAS ART
HA.com/TexasArt

**Atlee Phillips**, Ext. 1786
AtleeP@HA.com

### 20TH-CENTURY DESIGN
HA.com/Design

**Christina Japp**, Ext. 1247
CJapp@HA.com
**Nicholas Dawes**, Ext. 1605
NickD@HA.com

### VINTAGE & CONTEMPORARY PHOTOGRAPHY
HA.com/ArtPhotography

**Ed Jaster**, Ext. 1288
EdJ@HA.com

## HISTORICAL

### AMERICAN INDIAN ART
HA.com/AmericanIndian

**Delia Sullivan**, Ext. 1343
DeliaS@HA.com

### AMERICANA & POLITICAL
HA.com/Historical

**Tom Slater**, Ext. 1441
TomS@HA.com
**Marsha Dixey**, Ext. 1455
MarshaD@HA.com
**John Hickey**, Ext. 1264
JohnH@HA.com
**Michael Riley**, Ext. 1467
MichaelR@HA.com

### CIVIL WAR AND ARMS & MILITARIA
HA.com/CivilWar

**Dennis Lowe**, Ext. 1182
DennisL@HA.com

### HISTORICAL MANUSCRIPTS
HA.com/Manuscripts

**Sandra Palomino**, Ext. 1107
SandraP@HA.com

### RARE BOOKS
HA.com/Books

**James Gannon**, Ext. 1609
JamesG@HA.com
**Joe Fay**, Ext. 1544
JoeF@HA.com

### SPACE EXPLORATION
HA.com/Space

**John Hickey**, Ext. 1264
JohnH@HA.com
**Michael Riley**, Ext. 1467
MichaelR@HA.com

### TEXANA
HA.com/Historical

**Sandra Palomino**, Ext. 1107
SandraP@HA.com

## JEWELRY & TIMEPIECES

### FINE JEWELRY
HA.com/Jewelry

**Jill Burgum**, Ext. 1697
JillB@HA.com

### WATCHES & FINE TIMEPIECES
HA.com/Timepieces

**Jim Wolf**, Ext. 1659
JWolf@HA.com

## MUSIC & ENTERTAINMENT MEMORABILIA
HA.com/Entertainment

**Doug Norwine**, Ext. 1452
DougN@HA.com
**John Hickey**, Ext. 1264
JohnH@HA.com
**Garry Shrum**, Ext. 1585
GarryS@HA.com
**Jim Steele**, Ext. 1328
JimSt@HA.com
**Kristen Painter**, Ext. 1149
KristenP@HA.com

## NATURAL HISTORY
HA.com/NaturalHistory

**David Herskowitz**, Ext. 1610
DavidH@HA.com

## RARE STAMPS
HA.com/Stamps

**Harvey Bennett**, Ext. 1185
HarveyB@HA.com
**Steven Crippe**, Ext. 1777
StevenC@HA.com

## SPORTS COLLECTIBLES
HA.com/Sports

**Chris Ivy**, Ext. 1319
CIvy@HA.com
**Peter Calderon**, Ext. 1789
PeterC@HA.com
**Mike Gutierrez**, Ext. 1183
MikeG@HA.com
**Lee Iskowitz**, Ext. 1601
LeeI@HA.com
**Mark Jordan**, Ext. 1187
MarkJ@HA.com
**Chris Nerat**, Ext. 1615
ChrisN@HA.com
**Jonathan Scheier**, Ext. 1314
JonathanS@HA.com

## VINTAGE MOVIE POSTERS
HA.com/MoviePosters

**Grey Smith**, Ext. 1367
GreySm@HA.com
**Bruce Carteron**, Ext. 1551
BruceC@HA.com
**Isaiah Evans**, Ext. 1201
IsaiahE@HA.com

## TRUSTS & ESTATES
HA.com/Estates
**Mark Prendergast**, Ext. 1632
MPrendergast@HA.com

## CORPORATE & INSTITUTIONAL COLLECTIONS/VENTURES
**Jared Green**, Ext. 1279
Jared@HA.com

## AUCTION OPERATIONS
**Norma Gonzalez**, Ext. 1242
*V.P. Auction Operations*
Norma@HA.com

## CREDIT DEPARTMENT
**Marti Korver**, Ext. 1248
Marti@HA.com
**Eric Thomas**, Ext. 1241
EricT@HA.com

## MARKETING
**Debbie Rexing**, Ext. 1356
DebbieR@HA.com

## MEDIA & PUBLIC RELATIONS
**Noah Fleisher**, Ext. 1143
NoahF@HA.com

## HOUSTON OFFICE
**Mark Prendergast**
713-899-8364
MPrendergast@HA.com

## CORPORATE OFFICERS
**R. Steven Ivy**, Co-Chairman
**James L. Halperin**, Co-Chairman
**Gregory J. Rohan**, President
**Paul Minshull**, Chief Operating Officer
**Todd Imhof**, Executive Vice President
**Leo Frese**, Vice President

Dear Bidder,

Heritage is proud to be offering The Canadiana Collection, the finest condition collection of Canadian coins ever assembled, at our 2010 New York International Numismatic Convention event (an Official Auction of the NYINC and taking place at the Waldorf-Astoria in New York City).

The Canadiana Collection contains the finest quality coins (from the early issues of the Confederation through the mid-twentieth century) that we have ever seen. In fact, it contains more 'finest known" examples than any other Canadian collection ever formed! That is speaking volumes, as Heritage has sold several world famous collections of the coins of our Northern neighbors recently (including Belzberg, Dominion, and Wellington), as well as hundreds of individual rarities from the earlier Norweb and Pittman collections. Over our four decades in the rare coin business, we thought that we had seen it all in Canadian coinage – and we never expected to sell any comprehensive collection of rarities in finer condition than the stellar collections just mentioned.

As soon as we examined the exquisite rarities in the Canadiana Collection, we instantly knew that these were the best of the best. When collectors of Canadian coinage brag about pedigrees in the decades to come, the Canadiana name will be at the head of the top tier. We never expect to see another collection with as many finest known coins with so many distinguished pedigrees. As you would expect with one of the greatest collections ever assembled, every Canadian rarity is present (and here we will point out that the consignor kept a few of his treasures, so the auction is not complete). But here you will find all three 1936 "Dot" coins in the finest grades, the finest known 1890-H half dollar, a 1921 half dollar in MS66, and a 1921 five cents in MS 67. Perhaps the most impressive section is the astonishing offering of Victorian quarters and halves. Thirty years of effort have produced a collection of exceptional quality, of a level so consistent and so high as to almost be unbelievable. Yet it is there to be seen and to be appreciated. Please join us in New York and see if you don't agree!

If you will be participating from home, we encourage you to use either – or both – of our exclusive bidding platforms: the Interactive Internet™ and HERITAGE Live!™ You can also participate by telephone, mail, fax, or agent. Good luck, and have a wonderful 2010.


Greg Rohan
President
Heritage Auction Galleries

Warren Tucker
Director
World Coin Auctions

Cris Bierrenbach
Director of International Sales
World Coin Auctions

*America's Most Prestigious*
*Foreign & Ancient Coin Show*

**NYINC**
NEW YORK
**INTERNATIONAL**
NUMISMATIC
CONVENTION

The 38th Annual

# NEW YORK INTERNATIONAL
# NUMISMATIC CONVENTION

## JANUARY 8-10, 2010

**(Early Birds – Thursday, January 7: 2PM - 7PM – $100)**

### Public Show Hours:
Friday, January 8: 10AM - 7PM
Saturday, January 9: 10AM - 7PM
Sunday, January 10: 10AM - 3PM

$10 for a three-day pass valid Friday through Sunday - 16 and under free with an adult
(Check our Web site to print a discount admission coupon)

### Waldorf Astoria Hotel • 301 Park Avenue
(Between 49th and 50th Streets)

Call (212) 355-3000 and mention rate code "NYI" for our special NYINC room rates of $269 or $289
(Call early. Limited rooms available at these special discounts.)

• *Auctions:*
  * *Numismatik Lanz and Numismatica Bernardi S.R.L.: Monday, January 4*
  * *Heritage: Sunday and Monday, January 3-4*
  * *Freeman and Sear: Tuesday, January 5*
  * *Classical Numismatic Group: Tuesday and Wednesday, January 5-6*
  * *Baldwin's/ M&M Numismatics/ Dmitry Markov/ Fritz Kuenker:*
    *Wednesday and Thursday, January 6-7*
  * *Ponterio and Associates - a division of Bowers and Merena:*
    *Friday and Saturday, January 8-9*
  * *George Frederick Kolbe: Saturday, January 9*
  * *Gemini Numismatic Auctions: Sunday, January 10*

• *Bourse Information:*
  *Kevin Foley – Convention Chairman*
  *P.O. Box 370650, Milwaukee, WI 53237*
  *(414) 421-3484 • FAX: (414) 423-0343*
  *E-mail: kfoley2@wi.rr.com*

Visit our Web site, **www.nyinc.info,** for a complete Schedule of Events, including
auction lot viewing, auction sessions, educational programs and bourse hours.

# SESSION ONE
## THE CANADIANA COLLECTION
## HERITAGE SIGNATURE WORLD COIN AUCTION

Floor, Telephone, HERITAGE Live!, Internet, Fax, and, Mail Signature Auction #3008
Sunday, January 3, 2010, 4:00 PM ET, Lots 20001-20365
New York City

A 15% Buyer's Premium ($14 minimum) Will Be Added To All Lots
Visit HA.com to view full-color images and bid.

**20001** **Victoria Cent 1859 Narrow 9,** KM1, MS66 Red PCGS. Minute doubling is evident on the 185, but the 9 is normal. The reverse has a bold die crack inside the inner beaded circle, from 12 o'clock down to 8 o'clock, through the left upright of the N in ONE, and through the E in CENT. This incredible coin has brilliant orange mint color with frosty luster. The surfaces are pristine and nearly perfect. The Norweb Collection included several 1859 Cents, none better than MS65 Red and Brown. Similarly, the finest Dominion Collection example graded MS64 Red and Brown, and the finest Belzberg Collection coin graded MS64 Red. This incredible Premium Gem is the only MS66 that PCGS has certified regardless of color designation (7/09). It is probably the finest known example of the date.
*From the Canadiana Collection*
Estimate: $2,500-$3,500   Starting Bid: $1,250

## Singular MS66 Red 1887 Victoria One Cent

**20002 Victoria Cent 1887,** KM7, MS66 Red PCGS. Out of 1.5 million pieces struck, this is the sole highest-graded example certified by PCGS (7/09); not only is it the lone survivor awarded the MS66 designation by that service, but it retains fully Red surfaces, actually rich copper-gold and orange with peach overtones. Victoria's hair is finely wrought. Scattered small marks and tiny isolated areas of deeper color are visible on either side. A leading Canadian dealer had this to say about this piece, "It is the finest Victoria Cent, of any date, that I have ever seen." In sum, a rare opportunity to obtain a fantastic representative—the finest the issue has to offer.
*From the Canadiana Collection*
Estimate: $20,000-$30,000  Starting Bid: $10,000

**20003** **Edward VII Cent 1903,** KM8, MS65 Red PCGS. Bright orange mint color and frosty luster characterize this Gem. The surfaces have a few tiny abrasions and carbon flecks that prevent a higher grade. PCGS has certified eight pieces as MS65 Red, with none finer (7/09). The Belzberg Collection had an MS65 Red, as did the Norweb Collection; the Dominion Collection had an MS65 Brown.
*From the Canadiana Collection*
Estimate: $800-$1,200  Starting Bid: $400

**20004** **George V Cent 1911,** KM15, MS66 Red PCGS. The first year of issue for the George V Cents and a one-year type coin, without the Latin DEI GRATIA following the King's name. The frosty surfaces on this extraordinary Premium Gem display fiery orange mint luster. A single faint line is noted at the center reverse. PCGS has certified nine examples at this grade level, but none finer in any color category (7/09). The Norweb Collection had a Specimen 66 PCGS coin and a MS63. Several pieces in the Dominion Collection included a MS65 Red and Brown, and the Belzberg Collection had a MS64 Red.
*From the Canadiana Collection*
Estimate: $800-$1,200  Starting Bid: $400

**20005** **George V Cent 1912,** KM21, MS65 Red PCGS. After a public outcry over the so-called "Godless" coinage of 1911, new dies were created in 1912 with the DEI GRATIA motto restored, making this issue the first of the new design. A stunning beauty with blazing orange cartwheel luster on both sides, this Gem is boldly detailed with impressive surfaces. A tiny mark in the left obverse field precludes an even finer grade. The Belzberg Collection had a MS66 Red, while the Norweb and Dominion collections had MS65 Reds as finest.
*From the Canadiana Collection*
Estimate: $1,500-$2,000  Starting Bid: $750

**20006** **George V Cent 1915,** KM21, MS65 Red PCGS. Splashes of lilac toning enhance the eye appeal of this delightful Gem. A few tiny spots on each side are evident, as is typically seen on the bronze Cents. PCGS has only certified six examples in MS65 Red, with just one finer (7/09). The Norweb Collection had a MS65 Red and Brown example, previously King Farouk; the Dominion Collection had a MS62, and the Belzberg Collection had a MS65 Red, similar to the present piece. Fully brilliant Red Canadian large Cents are greatly underrated and appear to represent remarkable value at current market prices.
*From the Canadiana Collection*
Estimate: $1,750-$2,200  Starting Bid: $875

**20007** **George V Cent 1924,** KM28, MS65 Red PCGS. This example is one of just five full Red examples certified in all grades (7/09), and is the finest Mint State piece that PCGS has ever certified. The present opportunity is of major importance for the Canadian Cent specialist. This splendid Gem exhibits rich orange mint luster with exceptional eye appeal. Both sides have slight mellowing of the mint color. The date is rare and highly desirable, especially in such remarkable condition. The Norweb Collection had two pieces, a Specimen 65 Brown and a MS64 Brown. The Dominion Collection had a MS64 Red, and the Belzberg collection had a Specimen 65 Red.
*From the Canadiana Collection*
Estimate: $6,000-$7,500  Starting Bid: $3,000

**20008** **George V Cent 1936,** KM28, MS66 Red PCGS. Housed in a green-label holder, this impressive Cent has amazing orange mint color with frosty surfaces. A few tiny specks on each side are normal for the Cents of this era. An exceptional example representing the final year of the George V type, this piece will be a wonderful representative of the design in a high-quality type collection. Despite a mintage of more than 8 million coins, high-grade pieces remain elusive. A MS65 Red appeared in the Dominion Collection, previously from the Pittman sale, and a MS64 Red was featured in the Belzberg Collection, also from Pittman, and a cleaned MS60 represented the date in the Norweb Collection. This Premium Gem is tied with one other example as the finest that PCGS has ever graded (7/09).
*From the Canadiana Collection*
Estimate: $600-$800  Starting Bid: $300

## Legendary 1936 Dot Cent—Finest of Three Known

**20009 George V Cent 1936 Dot,** KM28, Specimen 66 Red PCGS, Ex: Belzberg. Amongst the most famous rarities in Canadian numismatics, struck in 1937 prior to the creation of coinage dies for George VI but never released for circulation, the 1936-dated Dot cent has seen its reputation grow exponentially since its discovery. It was long considered essentially uncollectible, since noted numismatist John Jay Pittman had held all three known examples from 1961 until his death, but the three-part auction of his collection brought all three back onto the market: the first in October 1997 and the other two (including this piece) in August 1999. The three 1936 Dot Cents, now well-scattered, generate great excitement whenever one appears on the auction block.

The description of this piece that appeared in the catalog for The John Jay Pittman Collection, Part Three, penned by David Akers, elegantly sums up the coin's attributes. It appears below:

**"One Cent, 1936. Dot below date. Gem Specimen.** Lightly lacquered at the Mint to preserve its original color and the quality of its surfaces. This objective has been achieved and the coin is basically 'as struck' with all of its original mint red color intact. This piece is fully struck with a sharp, fully mirrored edge and bold design details. There are a few areas of minor discoloration in the lacquer, but no impairments to the actual surfaces of the coin. The fields have many fine raised die scratches resulting from extensive polishing of the dies. This is by far the finest of three known examples and it could not be improved upon in any significant respect."

The only additional note this cataloger would make is that this piece is easily identified as having come from the complete Dot Specimen set. The best diagnostic is the thin streak in the lacquer that passes from the right reverse rim through the tip of the nearby maple leaf and into the space between ONE and CENT.

*Ex: T. Roberts, employee of the Royal Canadian Mint; Mrs. T. Roberts, widow of the preceding; John Jay Pittman, 1954, sold as part of the 1936 Dot Specimen set for $250; John Jay Pittman Collection, Part Three (David Akers, 8/1999), lot 2486a, uncertified, sold as part of the same set for $345,000; The Sid and Alicia Belzberg Collection of Canadian Coinage (Heritage, 1/2003), certified as Specimen 66 Red by PCGS, lot 15608, sold alone for $230,000. From the Canadiana Collection*
Estimate: $300,000-$400,000  Starting Bid: $150,000

**20010** **Victoria 5 Cents 1858 Small Date,** KM2, MS63 PCGS. The Small Date is the normally encountered variety of 1858, with examples relatively plentiful in circulated grades but scarce in Mint State. The digits in the date are small and widely spaced.

The obverse has frosty luster with slight central weakness and heavy clash marks in the fields, and the reverse is fully prooflike with prominent vertical lapping lines. The reverse was probably resurfaced to remove clash marks, although there is no loss of detail. The reverse has a die crack through the E in CENTS. PCGS has certified 13 in MS63 with 11 finer (7/09).
*From the Canadiana Collection*
Estimate: $500-$700   Starting Bid: $250

**20011** **Victoria 5 Cents 1858 Large Date over Small Date, RP-1,** KM2, MS65 PCGS, Ex: Mason Collection. Housed in a green-label holder, this Gem is the single finest Large Date piece that PCGS has certified (7/09). It also represents the important Large Date over Small Date variety. Repunching is visible on the 858, with the original digits smaller than the final digits. Other varieties are known with a repunched Large Date, where the digits all the same size. The *Charlton Catalogue* suggests that all examples with a repunched date are the Large over Small Date coins, although that appears to be incorrect. The Norweb Collection had a Large over Small date piece in MS63, along with two different Large Repunched Date coins that graded Specimen 64 and AU55. The Dominion Collection had an AU55, and the Belzberg Collection lacked an example of the Large over Small Date variety. This delightful Gem has fully prooflike surfaces beneath splendid ivory and blue toning. The surfaces are immaculate, and the eye appeal is first-rate. Fully original, and an impressive example of this condition rarity.
*From the Canadiana Collection*
Estimate: $8,000-$10,000   Starting Bid: $4,000

**20012** **Victoria 5 Cents 1870 Wide Rim,** KM2, MS64 ICG. ICG has incorrectly identified this as the Narrow Rim variety. The obverse has severe clash marks in the fields. The reverse has a die crack inside the wreath from the crown to the upright of E and the leaf tip just right of the 1, with branches to the 5 and to the 87. An impressive Choice Mint State example, this piece has brilliant silver luster with splashes of gold and steel toning on the obverse. The surfaces are satiny, with prominent raised die lines visible in the reverse fields. Slight central weakness is evident on both sides, with the peripheral details bold. The two border varieties appear to be about equal in availability.
*From the Canadiana Collection*
Estimate: $800-$1,000   Starting Bid: $400

**20013** **Victoria 5 Cents 1870 Wide Rim,** KM2, MS65 PCGS. The reverse has a fine die crack from the E in CENTS to the bottom left curve of the 8 and the ribbon bow. There is also a fine crack from the border to a leaf at 10 o'clock, and a heavy crack from the border to a leaf at 3 o'clock. The cracks are identical to the Dominion Collection coin, a pleasing MS63. An impressive Gem, this toned example has light gray color at the centers, with peripheral iridescent toning on both sides. The surfaces are smooth and original, indicating a history of careful preservation.
*From the Canadiana Collection*
Estimate: $2,500-$3,500   Starting Bid: $1,250

**20014** **Victoria 5 Cents 1871,** KM2, MS64 PCGS. Eight coins have received the MS64 PCGS grade, with only three finer coins (7/09). However, the 1871 is a great coin for the type collector, with the highest total PCGS population of any silver 5 Cent piece. There were two examples in the Dominion Collection, a MS64 that was from the Norweb Collection, and a MS63. The Belzberg Collection had two amazing MS65 coins, both previously featured in the Pittman Collection. Both sides of this near-Gem have impressive luster with full mint frost and faint traces of toning. The obverse has minor clash marks along with a heavy die crack left of the D of DEI and another through the E of REGINA. The reverse appears to be bulged, with strong centers and weaker peripheries.
*From the Canadiana Collection*
Estimate: $1,200-$1,500   Starting Bid: $600

**20015**  **Victoria 5 Cents 1872-H,** KM2, MS66 PCGS. An incredible condition rarity, this Premium Gem 1872-H is one of just two coins that PCGS has graded MS66. Both sides have frosty luster beneath mottled gold, russet, and steel toning, with exceptional design definition. Although unidentified as such, this is the Belzberg coin, lot 15175 in our January 2003 sale. At the time, we commented that this is one of the finest Victorian 5 Cent coins we have seen in Specimen or Mint State format. Recertified since that time, it is likely that this single coin accounts for both grading events on the *PCGS Population Report*. The only other examples of this issue that we have handled are a MS62 from the Dominion Collection and a Specimen 63 coin that was also in the Belzberg Collection. This stunning 5 Cent piece is a coin that will appeal to the connoisseur who appreciates pristine, original examples of the coiner's art.
*From the Canadiana Collection*
Estimate: $6,500-$8,500   Starting Bid: $3,250

**20016**  **Victoria 5 Cents 1874-H Large Date,** KM2, MS65 PCGS, Crosslet 4 in date. This offering is just the fourth of the Large Date variety that we have presented, the others grading MS64 (two) and Specimen 65. This piece is the single finest 5 Cent 1874-H Crosslet 4 piece that PCGS has certified—a remarkable example that may never yield to an upgrade (7/09). Faint clash marks are visible in the fields on both sides of this pristine silver coin. Both sides have bold design definition and brilliant silver luster beneath blue-green and iridescent toning.
*From the Canadiana Collection*
Estimate: $6,000-$7,000   Starting Bid: $3,000

**20017** **Victoria 5 Cents 1874-H Small Date,** KM2, MS65 PCGS, Plain 4 in date. The two 1874-H 5 Cent pieces in the present sale are the first two MS65 examples that we have ever offered, although we did offer a Specimen 65 in our Belzberg sale. PCGS has certified four submissions of this variety in MS65, but none finer (7/09). Tied for the finest certified at PCGS, the present example displays exceptional desirability. It is a fully original example with frosty light gray surfaces and a frame of deep russet, gold, and steel toning, with additional traces of turquoise and violet. This offering represents the fifth time that we have offered the Small Date variety. The earlier appearances graded XF, MS63, MS64, and Specimen 61.
*From the Canadiana Collection*
Estimate: $4,000-$5,000   Starting Bid: $2,000

**20018** **Victoria 5 Cents 1875-H Small Date,** KM2, MS64 PCGS. The size of the date distinguishes the two known varieties of 1875-H silver 5 Cent pieces. The maple leaf's left corner under the 5 is below the left side of the 5 on the Small Date, and below the center on the Large Date. The individual digits are all thicker and closer on the Large Date. The differences are slight, and difficult to distinguish without the two varieties side by side. The Large Date variety is scarcer than the Small Date, but both are extremely important rarities in the series. The 1875 issues are to the Victoria coinage what the 1921 coins are to the George V series.

This amazing Choice Mint State piece is fully brilliant, with frosty silver luster. A few faint splashes of darker toning are evident, while surface marks are entirely minimal. Both sides show extensive clash marks, and close examination reveals minute doubling of the mintmark. The Norweb example was MS63, and the Belzberg example was MS64. PCGS has only certified twelve Mint State 1875-H 5 Cents of both varieties, including a single MS65 and two other MS64 coins tied with this piece for second finest certified (7/09).
*From the Canadiana Collection*
Estimate: $8,000-$10,000   Starting Bid: $4,000

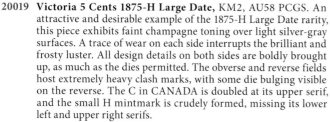

**20019 Victoria 5 Cents 1875-H Large Date,** KM2, AU58 PCGS. An attractive and desirable example of the 1875-H Large Date rarity, this piece exhibits faint champagne toning over light silver-gray surfaces. A trace of wear on each side interrupts the brilliant and frosty luster. All design details on both sides are boldly brought up, as much as the dies permitted. The obverse and reverse fields host extremely heavy clash marks, with some die bulging visible on the reverse. The C in CANADA is doubled at its upper serif, and the small H mintmark is crudely formed, missing its lower left and upper right serifs.

This near-Mint example is one of just three pieces graded as such at PCGS, with only two finer coins, both MS61 (7/09). The Norweb Collection had a Specimen 67, the Belzberg Collection had a Specimen 65 and a MS61, and the Dominion Collection had an AU55. Aside from the Belzberg and Dominion coins, we have only handled two others—a Fine 12 and a VF25.
*From the Canadiana Collection*
Estimate: $2,500-$3,500 Starting Bid: $1,250

**20020 Victoria 5 Cents 1880-H, Reverse 3,** KM2, MS65 PCGS. With a mintage of 3 million coins, the 1880-H ranks as an available date suitable for type collectors. However, PCGS has only certified four examples as MS65 with none finer (7/09), so this piece is the best available quality for the date and will appeal as much to specialists as type collectors. It is far finer than the Norweb Collection MS62 coin and the Dominion Collection MS63 example. It is also finer than the Pittman-Wellington coin, a MS64, and finer than the Belzberg MS64 example. The Belzberg Collection also had a Specimen 65 coin. This is the first MS65 we have ever offered, a landmark opportunity for the advanced collector. Both sides of this boldly defined Gem have satiny luster beneath grayish-gold toning with iridescent accents on each side. The surfaces are remarkably well preserved even for a MS65, with trivial abrasions only visible under magnification.
*From the Canadiana Collection*
Estimate: $3,500-$4,500 Starting Bid: $1,750

**20021 Victoria 5 Cents 1881-H,** KM2, MS66 PCGS. Here is an amazing representative of the date, considered common from a mintage of 1.5 million coins. Like the 1880-H in this sale, this piece is the finest available. PCGS has certified two submissions in MS66, with none finer (7/09). In fact, the next finest certified is only MS64. The Norweb Collection had two pieces, MS62 and AU58, the Dominion Collection had a MS63, and the Belzberg Collection had a Specimen 64 and a MS64. No Mint State pieces even close to this grade have appeared in our past auctions. This is an amazing opportunity to acquire the finest available quality piece. This Premium Gem has frosty luster with exceptional design definition. Both sides offer lovely medium gray toning. The obverse adds splashes of gold, lilac, and steel, with similar toning and a light ivory area on the reverse.
*From the Canadiana Collection*
Estimate: $5,000-$7,000   Starting Bid: $2,500

**20022 Victoria 5 Cents 1882-H,** KM2, MS66 PCGS. This issue marks the first year of a modified reverse design with 22 leaves. The extra leaf is on the outside of the right branch, second from the bottom. The 1882-H is a common date among Heaton Mint issues, with a mintage of 1 million coins. Quite a few survive, with nearly all certified pieces grading AU50 or finer. The present piece, however, is anything but common—the finest that PCGS has certified. In fact, it is the *only* MS66 that PCGS has handled—an amazing condition rarity. The Norweb coin graded MS64 and was called a "Notable Gem." The Dominion Collection had a MS62 and the Belzberg Collection had a MS65. None of those coins can match this piece for its phenomenal quality. Both sides have satiny and reflective fields with a lovely cameo appearance, especially on the obverse. All design motifs are sharply defined. The surfaces have light toning on the devices with deeper iridescence in the fields. An incredible opportunity for the specialist—one that may not repeat for many years to come.
*From the Canadiana Collection*
Estimate: $6,000-$8,000   Starting Bid: $3,000

**20023  Victoria 5 Cents 1883-H,** KM2, MS65 PCGS. This is only the fourth 1883-H 5 Cent silver piece that we have ever handled, and it is tied with two other submissions for the finest that PCGS has certified (7/09). Both sides of this Gem have brilliant and highly lustrous silver surfaces, and the obverse even has some peripheral gold toning. All design elements are sharp, although minor weakness is evident at the central obverse. Both sides have faint die cracks.
*From the Canadiana Collection*
Estimate: $7,000-$10,000   Starting Bid: $3,500

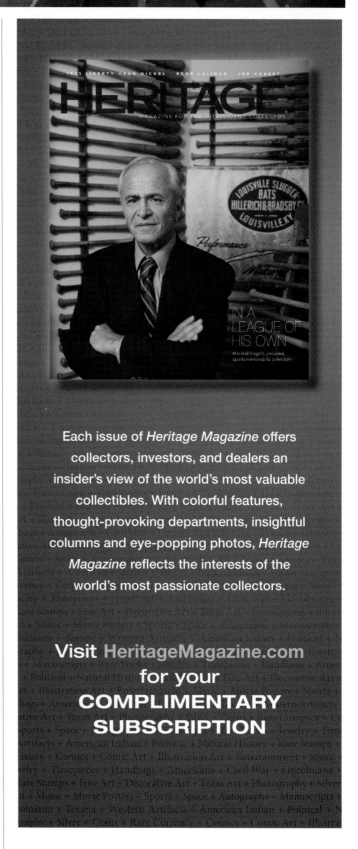

## Sensational Five Cents 1884 Near 4—Finest Certified

20024  **Victoria 5 Cents 1884 Near 4,** KM2, MS65 PCGS. Two major varieties, known as the Near 4 and Far 4, are extremely difficult to differentiate. A side-by-side comparison of photos suggests the following: the Near 4 has a thin upright to the 4, leaning to the left. The 1 in the date is distant from the leaf below, and the second 8 has an enlarged lower loop. The Far 4 has a heavy upright to the 4, and that digit is upright. The 1 is close to the leaf below, and the upper and lower loops of the second 8 are similar in size. The Near 4 has a pointed crosslet tip of the 4, while the Far 4 has a blunt tip. Both varieties are extremely rare in higher grades, while the Far 4 is scarcer in all grades.

This piece is an extraordinary Gem with fully original and beautiful toning over sharp design elements. Both sides have rich and vibrant gold, lilac, and sea-green toning over light ivory surfaces. The underlying mint luster is frosty and radiant. The Dominion Collection had a MS63 representative of this date. The Norweb coin was called MS64 in that catalog, and described as "far and away finer than any seen in recent times." Later, that same coin was PCGS certified as Specimen 65 and appeared in our Belzberg sale. This piece is the finest of just five Mint State 1884 Five Cent pieces that PCGS has graded (7/09) and the single finest certified of this key rarity. The present auction is rich in outright rarities and condition rarities in the Canadian series. Opportunities abound for the advanced Canadian specialist.
*From the Canadiana Collection*
Estimate: $25,000-$35,000  Starting Bid: $12,500

**20025  Victoria 5 Cents 1885 Small 5,** KM2, MS64 PCGS. This boldly detailed near-Gem has wispy gold toning over brilliant silver surfaces. Both sides have satiny luster with reflective fields. PCGS has certified five examples in MS64 with just four finer coins (7/09). The Norweb Collection lacked this variety, having two examples of the Large 5 instead. The Dominion Collection had a MS65 that was from Belzberg. A desirable and attractive silver 5 Cents.
*From the Canadiana Collection*
Estimate: $4,000-$5,000   Starting Bid: $2,000

**20026  Victoria 5 Cents 1885 Large 5,** KM2, MS66 PCGS. Two varieties are known as the Small 5 and Large 5 issues, with the Small 5 being slightly scarcer. A third variety has the small 5 over a large 5. The Small 5 reverse die was created from the same three-digit logotype punch used for the 1882-H, 1883-H, and 1884 pieces. A new logotype punch was then created for the Large 5 dies. The *Charlton Standard Catalogue* notes that the difference is a short top on the Small 5 and a large top on the Large 5. While those differences are easily distinguished, the prominent ball at lower left of the Large 5 and the missing ball at lower left of the Small 5 allow for an even more distinguished distinction between the two varieties.

This incredible Large 5 piece is the single finest example of the variety that PCGS has ever certified (7/09). It is finer than the Norweb MS64 coin, either of the Belzberg MS64 examples, and much finer than the Dominion Collection MS63 piece. Both sides have fully original light silver-gray and champagne surfaces with gorgeous iridescent toning. The 5 in the date shows evidence of recutting below, although different from the Small over Large 5 variety.
*From the Canadiana Collection*
Estimate: $12,000-$15,000   Starting Bid: $6,000

**20027 Victoria 5 Cents 1886 Small 6,** KM2, MS66 PCGS. The Small 6 variety is slightly more plentiful than the Large 6 when all grades are considered, but both are major rarities in Gem condition. In fact, PCGS has only certified one of each in MS65 or finer grades (7/09). This amazing MS66 coin is followed by five MS64 examples in the *PCGS Population Report,* while the MS65 1886 Large 6 piece in this sale is the only Gem of that variety that PCGS has certified. Both represent incredible opportunities for the specialized collector who may wish to keep them together for years to come. This sensational piece has frosty luster and bold design details beneath beautiful rose and blue toning on each side. The pristine surfaces approach perfection.
*From the Canadiana Collection*
Estimate: $5,500-$7,500   Starting Bid: $2,750

**20028 Victoria 5 Cents 1886 Large 6,** KM2, MS65 PCGS. A major rarity in the Canadian 5 Cents series, the 1886 Large 6 is seldom encountered in any grade. The mintage is unknown, although it was undoubtedly a tiny part of the 1.7 million coins struck that year. PCGS has only certified eight examples in all grades (7/09), the lowest population of any date or variety in the entire silver 5 Cents series.

Both the Norweb and Belzberg collections, for example, had two examples of the Small 6 variety—but no Large 6 piece. The Dominion Collection that we sold in September 2006 had a MS65 ICG example and our May 2006 sale had a MS64 PCGS coin. Those are the only two examples of the 1886 Large 6 Five Cents appearing in any of our past sales.

This sensational Gem displays pristine surfaces. Both sides have brilliant and frosty silver luster beneath turquoise, gold, and russet toning. Only a few trivial marks appear on the reverse. The overall appearance is entirely original, with outstanding aesthetic appeal. Faint clash marks are evident on the obverse, mostly above the Queen's head.

For the specialized collector, the opportunity to acquire such a monumental rarity must be grasped, since another chance to acquire this issue may be far in the future. This is the single finest PCGS-graded 1886 Large 6 Five Cents, and likely the finest existing example of the variety (7/09).
*From the Canadiana Collection*
Estimate: $6,000-$8,000   Starting Bid: $3,000

**20029 Victoria 5 Cents 1887,** KM2, MS65 PCGS, Ex: Belzberg Collection. Only 500,000 1887 5 Cents silver pieces were coined at the Royal Mint in 1887, resulting in a scarcer issue that is a rarity at the Gem level. This date is often overlooked in favor of more-famous rarities that are not as elusive in high grades. In addition to the present coin (the only one that PCGS has certified in MS65), PCGS has also graded two in MS66 (7/09). The Norweb coin was graded MS60, the Dominion Collection had two examples that graded MS64 and MS65, and the Belzberg Collection had an earlier appearance of the present piece. This gorgeous Gem has frosty luster shining through splendid gold and iridescent toning on both sides. It is entirely original and presents exceptional eye appeal. The design motifs are bold, and the overall desirability is of the highest order.
*From the Canadiana Collection*
Estimate: $2,500-$3,500   Starting Bid: $1,250

**20030 Victoria 5 Cents 1888,** KM2, MS66 PCGS. This boldly detailed Premium Gem is fully original, with exceptional mint frost on each side. Much of the obverse and reverse surfaces exhibit silver mint brilliance with rich gold and iridescent toning toward the peripheries. The surfaces are pristine, with only a few scattered, trivial marks. Slight recutting is visible below the final 8. PCGS has certified a single MS66 (this coin) along with one finer MS67. Behind these two are a single MS65 and a few MS64 and lower-grade coins. Considered a common date from a mintage of 1 million coins, this is one of many issues in the 5 Cents silver series that is elusive in Gem or finer grades. The Norweb Collection had two coins that graded MS62 and AU58. The Belzberg Collection had a MS64, and the Dominion Collection had a MS63. Prior to the current offering, the Belzberg MS64 was the finest Mint State example of this issue that we had handled. Here is an excellent opportunity for the advanced collector.
*From the Canadiana Collection*
Estimate: $3,000-$4,000   Starting Bid: $1,500

**20031** **Victoria 5 Cents 1889,** KM2, MS66 PCGS. The 1889 was the last year of the 22 Leaves Narrow Rim reverse before the change back to the 21 Leaves Narrow Rim reverse which resumed on the 1890 issue. The most difficult issue of the series, except for the 1885 Small 5/Large 5, and one that is increasingly rare in the higher grade levels. This charming Premium Gem is tied with one other piece for finest certified at PCGS (7/09). The essentially pristine surfaces offer hues of pinkish-gray, blue, and gold, with excellent eye appeal and a good strike overall. Minor strike weakness appears on the right-side reverse leaves.
*From the Canadiana Collection*
Estimate: $6,000-$8,000  Starting Bid: $3,000

**20032** **Victoria 5 Cents 1890H,** KM2, MS66 PCGS. In 1890, the earlier reverse type with only 21 leaves in the wreath reappeared after a nine-year intermission. From 1882 through 1889, the wreath had 22 leaves. On the present coin, the obverse has a broadly recut C in VICTORIA. Four of the five I's in the legend are defective: the first and second missing the upper right serif, the third missing the upper left serif, the fourth perfect, and the fifth with a strengthened upper left serif. This impeccable example has a bold strike with frosty silver luster and brilliant surfaces. Both sides have peripheral iridescence that is slightly heavier on the reverse. The surfaces are pristine and virtually mark-free. This example is one of two submissions that PCGS has certified as MS66, with none finer (7/09). The other MS66 appeared in our sale of the Belzberg Collection.
*From the Canadiana Collection*
Estimate: $2,500-$3,500  Starting Bid: $1,250

**20033 Victoria 5 Cents 1891 Obverse 5,** KM2, MS65 PCGS. This absolutely stunning Gem has brilliant silver centers with vibrant gold, blue, and iridescent peripheral toning. Both sides are well defined and show excellent peripheral and central detail. The obverse has satiny luster in the fields, while frosty devices provide a hint of cameo contrast. Produced to the extent of 1.8 million coins, this issue is considered a common date, but it is rare in Gem grade. PCGS has certified nine examples in MS65, with none finer (7/09). The Belzberg and Dominion collections each had a MS64; the Norweb Collection had an AU55.
*From the Canadiana Collection*
Estimate: $1,750-$2,200   Starting Bid: $875

**20035 Victoria 5 Cents 1893,** KM2, MS65 PCGS. Heather and pale-lime toning accompany the original light gray surfaces of this lustrous and sharply-defined Gem. Exceptional surfaces for the grade provide an outstanding presentation. PCGS has certified six examples in MS65, with none finer (7/09). The Dominion Collection had a MS63 previously in the Norweb Collection, and the Belzberg Collection had a MS64. It would be unfortunate for the specialist to miss this opportunity. Like so many others, the date is considered common, but the grade is uncommon.
*From the Canadiana Collection*
Estimate: $1,500-$1,800   Starting Bid: $750

**20034 Victoria 5 Cents 1892 Obverse 2,** KM2, MS66 PCGS. An extraordinary Premium Gem, this 1892 silver 5 Cents has fully lustrous silver surfaces beneath a thin coat of light gold toning. The surfaces are exceptional, with a few tiny marks only visible under magnification. Light clash marks are evident on the reverse. This beauty is tied with one other in MS66, and PCGS has also graded a single MS67 (7/09). This example is finer than any others offered recently. The Belzberg Collection had a MS65, the Dominion Collection had a MS63, and the Norweb Collection an AU55.
*From the Canadiana Collection*
Estimate: $3,500-$4,500   Starting Bid: $1,750

**20036 Victoria 5 Cents 1894,** KM2, MS64 PCGS, Ex: Dominion Collection. This impressive near-Gem is housed in an older green-label PCGS holder. Both sides are entirely brilliant, with exceptional mint frost. The designs are sharply brought up, and the quality is amazing for the grade. PCGS has certified six MS64 coins, two in MS65, and one in MS66 (7/09). This piece compares favorably with the Gem MS65 Norweb coin, and is similar to the MS64 example in the Belzberg Collection, and is one of the two from the Dominion Collection.
*From the Canadiana Collection*
Estimate: $2,000-$2,500   Starting Bid: $1,000

**20037** **Victoria 5 Cents 1896,** KM2, MS66 PCGS. A delightful jewel, this silver 5 Cents has intense mint frost beneath gray-gold, rose, and blue toning on both sides. The lustrous, pristine surfaces have no marks of any consequence. This piece is tied with two others for the finest that PCGS has certified (7/09), and it is finer than any recently offered. The Belzberg coin was MS65, the Dominion piece was MS62, and the Norweb example was AU58.
*From the Canadiana Collection*
Estimate: $2,500-$3,500   Starting Bid: $1,250

**20038** **Victoria 5 Cents 1897 Wide 8,** KM2, MS66 PCGS. The *Charlton Standard Catalogue* records three different varieties for 1897: the Wide 8, the Narrow 8, and the Narrow over Wide 8. The present Premium Gem is a Wide 8 that also shows slight repunching inside the upper loop of that digit, matching the Charlton plate for the variety. This boldly detailed piece is deeply toned with heather, gold, and pale-blue patina over frosty mint luster. One of just four PCGS-certified MS66 examples of the date (7/09).
*From the Canadiana Collection*
Estimate: $2,500-$3,500   Starting Bid: $1,250

**20039  Victoria 5 Cents 1898,** KM2, MS65 PCGS. With a mintage of just over 580,000 coins, the 1898 is a slightly scarcer date, and like so many others, it is a condition rarity in Gem grades. PCGS has certified three pieces in MS65 and just one finer MS66 coin (7/09). Light gold toning fails to subdue the brilliant underlying luster. The obverse has deeper gold, blue, and lilac toning near the border. A few scattered small ticks on the reverse require magnification to view. This piece is tied with the Belzberg piece, and is finer than either the Dominion or Norweb coins.
*From the Canadiana Collection*
Estimate: $2,500-$3,500   Starting Bid: $1,250

**20040  Victoria 5 Cents 1899,** KM2, MS65 PCGS. An absolutely amazing Gem with brilliant silver surfaces and bold design details on both sides, this piece lacks any trace of toning. The surfaces are impressive and virtually perfect. This example does not have toning; however, the surfaces are cleaner than similarly graded coins with toning. With a mintage of 3 million coins, this issue is considered common in all grades, but MS65 or finer coins are seldom encountered. PCGS has certified just six in MS65, and only four in higher grades (7/09).
*From the Canadiana Collection*
Estimate: $1,250-$1,500   Starting Bid: $625

**20041  Victoria 5 Cents 1900 Narrow 0,** KM2, MS66 PCGS. The Narrow 0 variety is the more common of two known varieties for 1900—the variety that date collectors usually pursue. This remarkable Premium Gem has frosty luster beneath original gray-gold toning, with accompanying sea-green and iridescent peripheries. All aspects of this piece, including its bold design elements, are exceptional. PCGS has certified four MS66 examples, with none finer (7/09). This piece is similar to the MS66 Norweb coin, and is finer than the MS65 examples in the Belzberg and Dominion collections.
*From the Canadiana Collection*
Estimate: $1,200-$1,500   Starting Bid: $600

**20043 Victoria 5 Cents 1901,** KM2, MS66 PCGS, Ex: Belzberg-Wellington. The final year of the Queen Victoria type, this Premium Gem has impeccable surfaces with outstanding gold, lime-green, and iridescent toning on both sides. The Queen died on January 22, 1901, and the coins of this date bearing her likeness provide a suitable commemorative of her life. A collection of the 1901 Queen Victoria coinage would serve as a fascinating collecting specialty. This example is one of just two PCGS MS66 coins that rank as the finest that service has ever examined (7/09).
*From the Canadiana Collection*
Estimate: $1,000-$1,300   Starting Bid: $500

**20044 Edward VII 5 Cents 1902,** KM9, MS67 PCGS. A sensational Superb Gem marking the introduction of the Edward VII design. King Edward's reign began when Queen Victoria died in January 1901, although her profile remained on the coinage through the end of that year. An amazing piece, this 1902 silver 5 Cents has brilliant white luster on both sides with delicate blue and gold toning along the borders. The design elements are boldly detailed, and the surfaces are immaculate. Because of a perceived engraving error, the public hoarded 1901 5 Cents pieces, only to find that no design change would be made. For that reason there are more surviving 1902s than any other date of the type. PCGS has certified eight MS67 examples, along with a single MS68 (7/09). The Belzberg, Dominion, and Norweb collections each had a MS67 representative.
*From the Canadiana Collection*
Estimate: $600-$800   Starting Bid: $300

**20045 Edward VII 5 Cents 1902-H Large H,** KM9, MS67 PCGS. This Superb Gem is the only such piece that PCGS has certified—the finest existing 1902-H Large H 5 Cents silver piece and much finer than other pieces that have crossed the auction block (7/09). The Norweb coin was MS65, the Belzberg coin was MS66, and the Dominion Collection example was MS64. The present piece is an amazing coin with frosty white luster on both sides and lovely peripheral gold and lilac toning. It is boldly detailed with incredible eye appeal. The collector will be challenged in the hunt for another example that is even close to this piece for overall grade and quality.
*From the Canadiana Collection*
Estimate: $900-$1,200   Starting Bid: $450

**20042 Victoria 5 Cents 1900 Wide 0,** KM2, MS66 PCGS. Over the years, the two varieties have been known by various names. PCGS refers to them as the Wide 0 and Narrow 0 varieties. The *Charlton Standard Catalogue* calls them the Large Date and Small Date varieties. They are also sometimes called the Oval 0s and Round 0s varieties. Regardless of what they are called, the Wide 0 variety is an important subset of the 1900 silver 5 Cents pieces. A splendid ivory-toned example, this Premium Gem exhibits lovely peripheral iridescence. Pristine surfaces and bold design features complete a pretty picture. This is the single finest PCGS example ever certified (7/09). The Belzberg Collection had a MS65 coin that later appeared in the Dominion Collection, and the Norweb Collection had a MS63.
*From the Canadiana Collection*
Estimate: $3,500-$4,500   Starting Bid: $1,750

**20046 Edward VII 5 Cents 1902-H Small H,** KM9, MS66 PCGS.
Small and Large Mintmark varieties are known for 1902
and they are easily distinguished. The Large H has four distinct serifs on the uprights while the Small H has no visible
serifs. This Small H variety is much more difficult to locate
and is seldom found in Gem quality. This piece is extraordinary with frosty luster and full mint brilliance on both sides.
Vibrant gold, blue, and iridescent peripheral toning accompanies faint champagne toning on both sides. PCGS has
certified six examples in MS66 and one in MS67 (7/09).
*From the Canadiana Collection*
Estimate: $900-$1,200   Starting Bid: $450

**20047 Edward VII 5 Cents 1903,** KM13, MS67 PCGS. The additional,
or 22nd, leaf appears outside the right branch, filling the large
open area just above the lowest leaf on the earlier 21-leaf design.
The 22-leaf reverse remained in use until the end of the silver 5
Cents series in 1921. This Superb Gem is housed in a green label
PCGS holder and is tied with two others for the finest certified
(7/09). Both sides have a delightful blend of gold, lime, and sea-
green toning over lustrous surfaces.
*From the Canadiana Collection*
Estimate: $0-up  No Minimum Bid

**20048 Edward VII 5 Cents 1903-H Small H,** KM13, MS64 PCGS. The
usual Small H mintmark variety. The year 1903 was a transi-
tional year for the 5 Cents silver design. All 1902 coins and the
1903-H coins had 21 leaves in the wreath. However, the 1903
Royal Mint coins had 22 leaves in the wreath. A note in the
*Charlton Standard Catalogue* discusses the situation: "In a move
unprecedented in Canadian coinage, the Royal Mint produced
a coin that bore a somewhat different design than that used by
its sub-contractor, Ralph Heaton, in 1903. The 1903 Royal Mint
issue features a new wreath with 22 instead of 21 leaves." This
Choice Mint State piece has wonderful gold and lilac toning
over satiny surfaces. The design details are bold and the surfaces are wonderful for the grade.
*From the Canadiana Collection*
Estimate: $1,500-$1,800   Starting Bid: $750

**20049 Edward VII 5 Cents 1904,** KM13, MS65 PCGS. Pleasing light
gray surfaces exhibit gold and blue-green toning over frosty silver
luster on both sides. The surfaces are pristine, save for trivial
marks hidden beneath the toning. This issue is slightly scarcer
than the common dates, and infrequently seen in the top grades.
PCGS has certified five in MS65 and just one finer MS66 (7/09).
The Belzberg and Dominion collections each had a MS64, and the
Norweb coin was only MS60.
*From the Canadiana Collection*
Estimate: $2,000-$3,000   Starting Bid: $1,000

**20050** **Edward VII 5 Cents 1905,** KM13, MS67 PCGS. The 1905 had a mintage of 2.6 million coins and is considered common in all grades. However, the present coin is the only MS67 that PCGS has ever certified (7/09). The strike is bold and the surfaces are frosty with mostly silver brilliance and peripheral blue, green, lilac, and gold accents. The immaculate surfaces are free of marks, even under a glass. The Norweb Collection had a MS65, and the Dominion and Belzberg Collections each had a MS64. The present piece is almost certainly the finest existing 1905 silver 5 Cents.
*From the Canadiana Collection*
Estimate: $2,000-$3,000   Starting Bid: $1,000

**20051** **Edward VII 5 Cents 1906,** KM13, MS65 PCGS. This lovely Gem is housed in an older green-label PCGS holder. Both sides have silver-gray toning over lustrous surfaces, with deep gold and iridescent toning. Just five MS65 examples are PCGS-certified, with only two finer MS66 pieces (7/09). This piece is equal to the Norweb MS65 and finer than the Belzberg MS64 or the Dominion MS63. The specialist who decides to pass on this coin in lieu of a MS66 may have a long wait to complete the collection.
*From the Canadiana Collection*
Estimate: $2,000-$3,000   Starting Bid: $1,000

**20052** **Edward VII 5 Cents 1907,** KM13, MS67 PCGS. This gorgeous Superb Gem exhibits frosty mint brilliance beneath lovely gold, blue, and green toning; the reverse is brighter with heavy die polishing lines in the upper field. The strike is bold, and the aesthetic appeal is exceptional. This is the single finest 1907 5 Cents that PCGS has certified (7/09). It is far finer than the Dominion Collection MS63 coin and handily outpaces the Belzberg MS64. The Norweb Collection had a coin graded MS67 as part of a group lot.
*From the Canadiana Collection*
Estimate: $1,500-$1,800   Starting Bid: $750

**20053** **Edward VII 5 Cents 1908 Small 8,** KM13, MS65 PCGS. This lovely Gem is housed in an older green label PCGS holder. All design elements are boldly detailed, and the surfaces exhibit frosty mint luster beneath rich champagne and gold toning. A few small marks on the crown are all that prevent a higher grade. PCGS has certified 13 examples in MS65, three of which are MS66 and three other are MS67 coins (7/09).
*From the Canadiana Collection*
Estimate: $500-$700   Starting Bid: $250

**20054** **Edward VII 5 Cents 1908 Small 8,** KM13, MS67 PCGS. This Superb Gem is one of three Small 8 pieces that PCGS has certified as MS67 (7/09). The bold strike accompanies frosty mint luster. The obverse has light gray and heather toning with peripheral sea-green. The reverse is mostly rose and turquoise with splashes of light yellow. A delightful example with exceptional eye appeal. This is the finest piece that has crossed the auction block in quite some time and presents an outstanding opportunity for the advanced collector.
*From the Canadiana Collection*
Estimate: $1,500-$1,800   Starting Bid: $750

**20055** **Edward VII 5 Cents 1909 Pointed Leaves,** KM13, MS64 PCGS. Also known as the Holly Leaves variety, this Choice Mint State piece is housed in an older green label PCGS holder. PCGS has certified eight of these in MS64 with one MS65 and one MS66 (7/09). This example has satiny silver surfaces with light gold and russet toning concentrated along the obverse border. The Belzberg Collection had a similar MS64, the Dominion Collection had a MS63, and the Norweb Collection also had a MS63. Amongst the 1909 Five Cents, the Pointed Leaves variety is much rarer, but the opposite is true of the 1910 Five Cents where the Round Leaves variety is rarer.
*From the Canadiana Collection*
Estimate: $2,000-$3,000   Starting Bid: $1,000

**20056  Edward VII 5 Cents 1909 Round Leaves,** KM13, MS67 PCGS. This Maple Leaves variety has bold design definition beneath a blend of gold, lime, russet, violet, and blue toning. The underlying surfaces have frosty luster, and the entire presentation is one of exceptional eye appeal for the toning enthusiast. This piece is one of three PCGS-certified as MS67 (7/09). The toning pattern and colors are similar to the Dominion and Wellington coins, both also graded MS67. The Belzberg coin was a MS67 as well, and, like the others, had a similar toning pattern. The similarity of four different high-grade coins suggests they may all have come from the same source.
*From the Canadiana Collection*
Estimate: $2,000-$3,000   Starting Bid: $1,000

**20057  Edward VII 5 Cents 1910 Pointed Leaves,** KM13, MS66 PCGS. This incredible example of the 1910 Holly Leaves is a fully brilliant Premium Gem with frosty silver luster and no evidence of toning. It is boldly defined with exceptional surfaces that exhibit only the tiniest marks on each side. PCGS has certified five in MS66, six in MS67, and a single MS68 (7/09).
*From the Canadiana Collection*
Estimate: $750-$1,000   Starting Bid: $375

**20058  Edward VII 5 Cents 1910 Round Leaves,** KM13, MS66 PCGS. From the year of Edward VII's death. Much more elusive than its 1910 Pointed (Holly) Leaves cousin in all grades, and the key to the Edward VII series along with the 1909 Pointed Leaves. Fully lustrous under a coating of pinkish-gold patination accented with blue near the rims. Tied for finest at PCGS with two other pieces, one of which was the Belzberg example.
*From the Canadiana Collection*
Estimate: $4,500-$5,500   Starting Bid: $2,250

**20059  George V 5 Cents 1911,** KM16, MS66 PCGS. The final type of the 5 Cents silver coinage was introduced in 1911, featuring the likeness of King George V on the obverse. He was crowned upon the death of Edward VII on May 6, 1910. An impressive Premium Gem with bold details. The obverse has delicate gold, blue, and violet toning, while the reverse is essentially brilliant with wispy champagne toning. Popular as a special one-year type issue sometimes called the "Godless" type or alternatively the "atheist" design, this example is one of 29 pieces that PCGS has certified MS66, with six finer MS67 coins (7/09).
*From the Canadiana Collection*
Estimate: $300-$500  Starting Bid: $150

**20060  George V 5 Cents 1912,** KM22, MS65 PCGS. This boldly detailed Gem has light gold toning over frosty silver luster. With exceptional eye appeal, this lovely 5 Cents is a coin that the connoisseur will appreciate. PCGS has certified ten in MS65, with just five finer MS66 coins (7/09).
*From the Canadiana Collection*
Estimate: $600-$800  Starting Bid: $300

**20061  George V 5 Cents 1913,** KM22, MS66 PCGS. This Premium Gem is housed in a green label PCGS holder. It is boldly detailed and highly attractive. The central obverse and reverse areas are brilliant with a frame of lovely rose and gold toning. PCGS has certified 25 in MS66 but only one finer coin in MS67 (7/09). The Norweb family could do no better than AU55, while the Dominion Collection had a MS65. The Belzberg coin is similar to this piece, graded MS66 PCGS.
*From the Canadiana Collection*
Estimate: $500-$700  Starting Bid: $250

**20062  George V 5 Cents 1914,** KM22, MS64 PCGS, Ex: Pittman-Belzberg. The 1914 silver 5 Cents issue is scarce and usually found in lower grades. The Belzberg Collection had two MS64 pieces, the Dominion Collection had a MS64, the Wellington Collection had a MS65, and the Norweb Collection had a MS60. This near-Gem is deeply toned, especially on the obverse where central rose toning is encircled by blue, green, and yellow. The reverse has brilliant silver luster inside the wreath with peripheral russet, lilac, blue, and amber.
*From the Canadiana Collection*
Estimate: $300-$500  Starting Bid: $150

**20063  George V 5 Cents 1915,** KM22, MS67 PCGS. A sensational Superb Gem, this 1915 is fully brilliant with silver-white surfaces, frosty luster, bold design details, and no toning on either side. The surfaces are remarkably well preserved, even at this lofty grade. This important 5 Cents piece is one of just two MS67 coins that PCGS has certified (7/09). It is finer than the Belzberg MS66, the Norweb MS64, and the Dominion MS63.
*From the Canadiana Collection*
Estimate: $3,500-$4,000  Starting Bid: $1,750

**20064** **George V 5 Cents 1916,** KM22, MS65 PCGS, Ex: Dominion Collection. Subtle gold toning is evident over the brilliant white-silver surfaces of this lovely Gem. Both sides have satiny luster and sharp design motifs. PCGS has certified nine MS65 coins, three MS66s, and one MS67 (7/09).
*From the Canadiana Collection*
Estimate: $1,200-$1,500   Starting Bid: $600

**20065** **George V 5 Cents 1917,** KM22, MS66 PCGS. This amazing Premium Gem is tied for the finest that PCGS has certified—one of 14 so graded (7/09). Both sides have frosty white luster with wispy gold toning. The surfaces are virtually mark-free. An outstanding example for the specialist.
*From the Canadiana Collection*
Estimate: $500-$700   Starting Bid: $250

**20066** **George V 5 Cents 1918,** KM22, MS65 PCGS. This frosty Gem has a few faint splashes of darker color, but the surfaces are essentially brilliant and white. Slight design weakness is evident at the center obverse, but the balance is sharply defined. A lovely example that is one of sixteen MS65 coins that PCGS has certified, along with four MS66 pieces (7/09).
*From the Canadiana Collection*
Estimate: $500-$700   Starting Bid: $250

**20067** **George V 5 Cents 1919,** KM22, MS66 PCGS. A boldly defined Premium Gem, this 1919 Five Cents piece has light gold toning over frosty silver luster on the obverse. The reverse is brilliant and untoned. A few surface marks are consistent with the grade. PCGS has certified nine in MS66 and three in MS67 (7/09).
*From the Canadiana Collection*
Estimate: $600-$800   Starting Bid: $300

**20068** **George V 5 Cents 1920,** KM22a, MS66 PCGS. Highly lustrous and well struck with splashes of light champagne toning over frosty silver surfaces. Light die cracks are evident on each side. Tied for the finest that PCGS has certified and equal to the Pittman-Belzberg coin. The Norweb family had a MS66 that was part of a group lot.
*From the Canadiana Collection*
Estimate: $700-$900   Starting Bid: $350

## The 'Prince of Canadian Coinage'—Classic 1921 5 Cents

**20069  George V 5 Cents 1921,** KM22a, MS67 PCGS. The 1921 Canada 5 Cents silver piece ranks high on a list of the greatest Canadian rarities. Such a list might include the 1936 Dot Cent and 10 Cents, the 1906 Small Crown 25 Cents, the 1921 50 Cents, the 1948 Dollar, and the 1916-C Sovereign, among others including many pattern issues. Some have nicknamed this issue the "Prince of Canadian Coins" on the heels of the 1921 50 Cents piece that is dubbed the "King of Canadian Coins."

The mintage for this issue exceeded 2.5 million coins. However, that figure does not explain the rarity. After legislation was passed to create a new 5 Cents piece of a copper and nickel composition, orders were issued to melt the older 5 Cents silver coins, with more than 3 million pieces melted, including nearly the entire 1921 mintage. Those that escaped the melting pot included some that entered circulation and others that collectors must have preserved, as examples are known in grades ranging from VG to Superb Gem. The number known today probably approaches 100 coins, if current population data is any indication. NGC and PCGS have graded a total of 87 pieces in all grades, a figure that includes resubmissions.

This amazing piece is by far the finest 1921 5 Cents silver piece that exists, to the best of our knowledge. It is the single finest piece that PCGS has ever certified (7/09)—a Superb Gem with light silver and pale heather patina, enhanced by splashes of translucent blue and iridescent toning. Only a trace of strike weakness is noted on the obverse.
*From the Canadiana Collection*
Estimate: $90,000-$120,000  Starting Bid: $45,000

**20070** **George V 5 Cents 1922,** S near rim, KM29, MS65 PCGS, Ex: Pittman. The first year of the 5 Cents nickel coins and quite elusive in Gem grades, this pleasing piece has a nice strike and frosty nickel-gray luster. PCGS has only certified one finer business strike (7/09). As a point of comparison, the Norweb Collection had a Specimen 64 coin and a MS63 that was offered as part of a group lot. We offered a MS65 in our January 2008 auction and another in our sale of the Dominion Collection—the only two previous appearances of a Gem Mint State coin in any of our sales.
*From the Canadiana Collection*
Estimate: $600-$800   Starting Bid: $300

**20071** **George V 5 Cents 1923,** KM29, MS65 PCGS. This is the finest Mint State example we have handled. The Norweb coin graded MS63, Belzberg had a Specimen 64 example, and the Dominion Collection had a MS63. A brilliant and fully lustrous Gem in a green-label holder, this piece has excellent design definition. This is an extremely difficult date to locate in Gem grades. PCGS has only certified seven in MS65, with just one finer (7/09).
*From the Canadiana Collection*
Estimate: $1,200-$1,500   Starting Bid: $600

**20072** **George V 5 Cents 1924,** KM29, MS66 PCGS. This is the only MS66 example that PCGS has graded, the finest Mint State 1924 Five Cents (7/09). An extraordinary example with highly lustrous and satiny gray surfaces, bringing out the exceptional design details on both sides. Belzberg had a Specimen 67 coin, while the Norweb coin was MS64, and the Dominion Collection coin was just MS63. Many of the so-called "common date" coins in the present collection are found in amazing condition, providing specialists and Canadian aficionados with countless opportunities to acquire the finest available coins.
*From the Canadiana Collection*
Estimate: $2,000-$3,000   Starting Bid: $1,000

**20073  George V 5 Cents 1925,** KM29, MS65 PCGS. Only 201,921 coins were minted, the lowest production total of the type. Other than 1926 with a mintage just under 1 million coins, every other date from 1922 to 1936 had a mintage in excess of 2 million coins. An important rarity in the Canadian 5 Cent nickel series, this Gem is one of just two MS65 pieces that PCGS has certified, with none finer (7/09). The Belzberg Collection had a Specimen 67 and a MS64, and the Norweb Collection had a Specimen 67 and a MS60. The Pittman Collection had four pieces, grading VG to Fine. This satiny Gem has fully lustrous light gray surfaces with some original planchet marks evident in the fields, as struck. There is no indication of any later abrasions.
*From the Canadiana Collection*
Estimate: $10,000-$12,000   Starting Bid: $5,000

**20074  George V 5 Cents 1926 Near 6,** KM29, MS66 PCGS, Ex: Belzberg. Following on the heels of the rare 1925 5 Cents, only 938,162 pieces were minted in 1926, including both Near 6 and Far 6 varieties. This incredible example from the Belzberg Collection is the only MS66 that PCGS has certified, the finest graded 1926 5 Cents piece (7/09). The Belzberg Collection also contained a Specimen 65 piece. The Norweb Collection had a Specimen 66 piece but no Mint State example, and the Dominion Collection had a MS64.
*From the Canadiana Collection*
Estimate: $7,500-$10,000   Starting Bid: $3,750

## Prized 1926 5 Cents Far 6

**20075 George V 5 Cents 1926 Far 6,** KM29, MS65 PCGS. The two rarest George V 5 Cents pieces are the 1925 and 1926 Far 6, the former important as a date and the latter as a variety. The reported mintage for all 1926 5 Cents pieces was 938,162 coins, although the breakdown between Near 6 and Far 6 coins is unknown. Examination of combined NGC and PCGS population totals for all grades suggests that the 1926 Far 6 coins are more elusive than the 1925 5 Cents. The two grading services have certified 161 of the former and 236 of the latter. The data suggests a production of about 135,000 examples of the 1926 Far 6 coins.

An amazing Gem, this 1926 Far 6 nickel is extremely rare in such high grades. PCGS has only certified three MS65 pieces, including this coin, with none finer. In all Mint State grades, the total PCGS population is only 18 coins, the lowest population of any George V 5 Cent piece. This boldly detailed Gem is highly lustrous, with satiny gray surfaces and faint champagne toning to enhance its eye appeal. The Belzberg coin was MS63 and the Dominion Collection piece was MS64. The Norweb Collection had a VF example. In our own Permanent Auction Archives, we record the Dominion and Belzberg coins as the top examples we have auctioned prior to this offering. The present opportunity is extremely important and should be met with enthusiasm. The new owner will prize this incredible piece for years to come.
*From the Canadiana Collection*
Estimate: $25,000-$35,000 Starting Bid: $12,500

**20076  George V 5 Cents 1927,** KM29, MS66 PCGS. An outstanding example, this beauty has satiny light gray luster beneath delightful pale champagne toning. The only shortcoming is a slightly weak strike, but every other aspect is outstanding. The Belzberg Collection had a Specimen 64, and the Norweb Collection had a MS60. This piece and one other PCGS MS66 coin are tied for the finest that service has ever graded (7/09). Before this appearance, the best we had offered was the MS64 Dominion Collection coin that we sold in September 2006. The specialist may wait many years for another opportunity to acquire the finest known example.
*From the Canadiana Collection*
Estimate: $2,500-$3,500  Starting Bid: $1,250

**20077  George V 5 Cents 1928,** KM29, MS66 PCGS. This beauty is one of just three PCGS-certified MS66 examples of the date, with none graded higher (7/09). It is fully lustrous and sharply defined with frosty gray surfaces. The delicate champagne color on each side trumps the minor dark toning splashes along the borders. Here is another extremely important issue in the George V series, far surpassing the AU58 coin in the Norweb Collection. Belzberg had a Specimen 64 but no Mint State piece. Two MS65 coins appeared in our September 2006 sale, from the Dominion and Wellington collections.
*From the Canadiana Collection*
Estimate: $1,500-$2,000  Starting Bid: $750

**20078  George V 5 Cents 1929,** KM29, MS65 ICCS. An outstanding example, this Gem is highly lustrous, with frosty gray brilliance and faint traces of champagne toning. All design elements are boldly defined, and the eye appeal is first-rate. The Norweb Collection had a MS64 and Belzberg had a Specimen 66. A similar MS65 ICCS coin was offered in our September 2006 Dominion Collection sale.
*From the Canadiana Collection*
Estimate: $1,500-$1,800  Starting Bid: $750

20079 **George V 5 Cents 1930,** KM29, MS66 PCGS. A stunning example, this MS66 has fully brilliant, satiny nickel-gray surfaces with wisps of champagne toning. The obverse is a trifle weak, but the reverse is boldly defined. Here is another extraordinary opportunity as the only MS66 that PCGS has ever certified, with none finer (7/09). The Norweb Collection offered a MS65, while Belzberg had an amazing Specimen 68 but no Mint State example. The example in the Dominion Collection was only MS63.
*From the Canadiana Collection*
Estimate: $2,500-$3,500  Starting Bid: $1,250

20080 **George V 5 Cents 1931,** KM29, MS65 PCGS. This beautiful Gem has satiny light gray luster with reflective fields and bold design motifs, although slight weakness appears at the lower reverse. The Belzberg Collection had a Specimen 67, the Dominion Collection had a MS63, and the Norweb Collection had an AU58. An elusive date, the 1931 5 Cents is conditionally rare in Gem or finer grades. PCGS has certified two MS65 coins and one MS67, the only example finer than this piece (7/09).
*From the Canadiana Collection*
Estimate: $2,000-$3,000  Starting Bid: $1,000

**20081** **George V 5 Cents 1932,** KM29, MS67 PCGS, Ex: Pittman. This important 5 Cents nickel is the only MS67 that PCGS has certified; the next finest is MS64 (7/09). We feel that it is the single finest Mint State 1932 5 Cents in existence. Even David Akers graded the coin a Gem in the Pittman catalog. He wrote: "In the Gem condition of this piece it is a decidedly rare item. This is surely one of the finest known examples of the issue and one could search far and wide and over a long period of time to find a comparable quality 1932 5 Cents." In November 2006 we handled one of the MS64 coins—the only other Mint State 1932 5 Cents appearing in our auction archives. The Belzberg Collection had a Specimen 67 coin, and the Norweb Collection could do no better than MS60. This remarkable representative is fully brilliant, with satiny luster and reflective fields. The bold strike imparts exquisite design definition. The surfaces are pristine, with aesthetic appeal second to none.
*From the Canadiana Collection*
Estimate: $12,000-$15,000   Starting Bid: $6,000

**20082** **George V 5 Cents 1933,** KM29, MS65 PCGS, Ex: Dominion. This splendid Gem has full satin luster with exceptional design details. The surfaces exhibit light gray mint brilliance. Housed in a green-label holder, this Gem is tied with three others for the finest that PCGS has graded (7/09). The Belzberg coin was MS64, and that piece reappeared in the Dominion Collection sale as part of the Wellington Collection. This coin is the Dominion offering that graded MS65, and the Norweb coin was MS62. In most instances, the current collection exceeds any of the past sales for grade, in some cases substantially so.
*From the Canadiana Collection*
Estimate: $3,000-$4,000   Starting Bid: $1,500

**20083** **George V 5 Cents 1934,** KM29, MS66 PCGS. A frosty Premium Gem, this lovely 5 Cents has hints of champagne color over fully brilliant and lustrous light gray surfaces. The strike is above average, and the overall eye appeal is excellent. PCGS has only certified two MS66 examples, with none finer (7/09). This piece far exceeds the Norweb MS64 and the Dominion Collection MS63. The Belzberg Collection included an amazing Specimen 68 coin, but no business strike.
*From the Canadiana Collection*
Estimate: $2,500-$3,500   Starting Bid: $1,250

**20084** **George V 5 Cents 1935,** KM29, MS65 ICCS. A sharp strike and satiny surfaces are immediately evident on this lovely Gem 5 Cents. Both sides have lustrous, light gray surfaces that are free of the usual abrasions. A few tiny surface ticks are inconsequential. For comparison purposes, PCGS has certified six examples as MS65 and none finer (7/09). One of those coins was offered in the Belzberg Collection, Otherwise, the Dominion Collection had a MS62, and the Norweb coin was only MS60.
*From the Canadiana Collection*
Estimate: $1,500-$1,800   Starting Bid: $750

**20085** **George V 5 Cents 1936,** KM29, MS65 ICCS. This impressive Gem has remarkable light gray surfaces with satiny luster. The fields exhibit faint die polishing lines. Trivial surface marks are of no concern on this beauty. PCGS has certified ten Gem MS65 coins and just four finer pieces (7/09). Past offerings included a Specimen 65 in the Belzberg Collection, a MS65 in the Norweb Collection, and another MS65 in the Dominion Collection. This date is an excellent choice for the type collector.
*From the Canadiana Collection*
Estimate: $750-$1,000   Starting Bid: $375

**20086** **George VI 5 Cents 1937,** KM33, MS65 ICCS. First year of issue for the new George VI design with the Beaver reverse. The new obverse design was by T. Humphrey Paget, the reverse by George Edward Kruger-Gray. This delightful Gem has fully brilliant light gray surfaces with frosty luster. The quality is exceptional for the grade. No Mint State pieces appeared in the Norweb or Belzberg collections, and the Dominion Collection had a MS64 offered in a group lot. Only a couple of dozen Gems have been certified, and finer pieces are extremely rare.
*From the Canadiana Collection*
Estimate: $200-$400  No Minimum Bid

**20087** **George VI 5 Cents 1938,** KM33, MS65 PCGS. A sharply struck representative, this Gem is brilliant and highly lustrous with satiny gray surfaces. A few scattered marks are mostly evident on the obverse. Here is a "common date" that is anything but common in Gem Mint State grades. PCGS has certified only four pieces as MS65, and they have never seen a finer example (7/09). The Norweb coin was MS65, the Dominion piece was MS64, and the Belzberg example was MS62.
*From the Canadiana Collection*
Estimate: $5,000-$7,000   Starting Bid: $2,500

**20088** **George VI 5 Cents 1939,** KM33, MS66 PCGS. A faint trace of champagne toning is evident over the frosty light gray surfaces of this outstanding example. Both sides are nicely defined. PCGS has certified eleven pieces in MS65, with nine finer (7/09). The Dominion Collection had a MS66, the Norweb Collection had a MS65, and the Belzberg collection had a MS64.
*From the Canadiana Collection*
Estimate: $350-$550   Starting Bid: $175

**20089** **George VI 5 Cents 1940,** KM33, MS65 ICCS. Delicate gold toning is especially evident on the reverse of this brilliant Gem. The frosty light gray surfaces are fully lustrous, and the design motifs are boldly rendered. While this coin is ICCS-certified, a comparison shows that PCGS has graded just five MS65 coins with none finer (7/09). This example is clearly finer than the Norweb MS64, and much nicer than the Belzberg and Dominion MS63 coins.
*From the Canadiana Collection*
Estimate: $1,000-$1,300   Starting Bid: $500

**20090** **George VI 5 Cents 1941,** KM33, MS65 PCGS. This sensational Gem has frosty light gray surfaces with brilliant mint luster. Wispy champagne toning adds to the overall eye appeal. PCGS has only certified three examples as MS65 with none finer (7/09). The Norweb Collection had a MS64, and the Dominion and Belzberg collections each had a MS63.
*From the Canadiana Collection*
Estimate: $1,750-$2,200   Starting Bid: $875

**20091** **George VI 5 Cents 1942 Nickel,** KM33, MS65 ICCS. Struck early in the year before the transition to the Tombac composition, this lovely 5 Cents has brilliant nickel-gray surfaces with frosty luster. Both sides have the usual scattered surface marks that are consistent with the grade. This piece is equivalent to the Norweb and Belzberg MS65 coins, and finer than the Dominion MS63 example. For comparison, PCGS has only graded eleven of these in MS65, with just two finer (7/09).
*From the Canadiana Collection*
Estimate: $500-$700   Starting Bid: $250

**20092  George VI 5 Cents 1942 Tombac,** KM39, MS65 ICCS. The War World II Tombac composition imparts a brilliant yellow-orange appearance to this delightful Gem. Both sides have full mint luster with frosty surfaces. Trivial marks and specks on each side are inconsequential. The finest PCGS-certified coins are three MS65 examples that are comparable to this ICCS piece (7/09).
*From the Canadiana Collection*
Estimate: $200-$400  No Minimum Bid

**20093  George VI 5 Cents 1943 Tombac,** KM40, MS65 ICCS. The Victory reverse was introduced in 1943, the large V doubling as an indication of the 5 Cents denomination. A sharp strike ensures that all design elements are boldly detailed, with a prooflike obverse and satiny reverse. Both sides have lemon-yellow color with rich orange and iridescent toning. For a population comparison, PCGS has certified five in MS65 and one finer (7/09).
*From the Canadiana Collection*
Estimate: $200-$400  No Minimum Bid

**20094  George VI 5 Cents 1944 No Chrome,** KM40a, MS66 PCGS. The planchet missed the chrome-plating process and exhibits highly lustrous light-gray brilliance, similar to the normal-composition nickel 5 Cents pieces. Faint champagne toning enhances the eye appeal of this important coin. The surfaces are immaculate and the strike is bold. The Dominion Collection had a similar MS65 example that was missing the chrome-plating.
*From the Canadiana Collection*
Estimate: $200-$300  No Minimum Bid

**20095  George VI 5 Cents 1945 Steel,** KM40a, MS67 PCGS. Highly lustrous ice-blue surfaces present exceptional eye appeal on this sharply defined Superb Gem. Heavy die polish is evident, giving satiny fields with a hint of cameo contrast. This coin is tied with four others for the finest that PCGS has certified (7/09) and it is finer than the Norweb MS66 coin.
*From the Canadiana Collection*
Estimate: $500-$800  Starting Bid: $250

**20096  George VI 5 Cents 1947,** KM39a, MS67 PCGS. A fully lustrous Superb Gem with amazing surfaces that are free of abrasions other than a few trivial marks on each side. Both sides exhibit satiny light gray luster and extremely sharp design features. This is the only MS67 that PCGS has certified—the finest of the variety (7/09).
*From the Canadiana Collection*
Estimate: $1,500-$1,800  Starting Bid: $750

**20097  George VI 5 Cents 1947 Dot,** KM39a, MS66 ICCS. Traces of strike doubling are evident on the obverse of this wonderful Premium Gem 5 Cents. Both sides have soft, frosty luster with light gray surfaces. The strike is excellent, and this piece possesses a full quota of eye appeal. For a population comparison, PCGS has certified seven MS66 coins and one finer (7/09). The Belzberg and Dominion collections each had a MS66, and the Norweb Collection had an AU58.
*From the Canadiana Collection*
Estimate: $1,750-$2,250  Starting Bid: $875

**20098  George VI 5 Cents 1947 Maple Leaf,** KM39a, MS66 PCGS, Ex: Dominion. Brilliant light gray surfaces and satiny luster accompany prooflike surfaces on this wonderful Gem. Most of the scattered marks on each side appear to remain from the original planchet, rather than post-strike imperfections. PCGS has certified five in MS66, with two finer (7/09).
*From the Canadiana Collection*
Estimate: $450-$650  Starting Bid: $225

**20099  George VI 5 Cents 1947 Maple Leaf,** KM39a, Specimen 66 PCGS, Ex: Wellington. Only two finer PCGS pieces have been certified, both Specimen 67 (7/09). This Premium Gem Specimen 5 Cents has fully mirrored light gray fields with extraordinary design definition on both sides. A few tiny lint marks and planchet flakes are visible, but there is no evidence of any post-production surface marks. PCGS has only certified two finer Specimen coins (7/09).
*From the Canadiana Collection*
Estimate: $350-$550  Starting Bid: $175

**20100** **George VI 5 Cents 1948,** KM42, MS66 PCGS, Ex: Dominion. A remarkable Premium Gem, this light gray example has brilliant satin luster and bold design definition. The surfaces have faint die polishing lines, creating a slight prooflike appearance. An outstanding example for the advanced specialist, this piece is tied for the finest that PCGS has certified (7/09).
*From the Canadiana Collection*
Estimate: $300-$500   Starting Bid: $150

**20101** **George VI 5 Cents 1949,** KM42, MS67 PCGS, Ex: Dominion. This flawless Superb Gem 5 Cents piece has essentially perfect light nickel-gray surfaces. Satiny luster is evident, with reflective fields and a hint of cameo contrast on each side. In addition to this Superb Gem, PCGS has certified two others in MS67, with none finer (7/09).
*From the Canadiana Collection*
Estimate: $750-$1,000   Starting Bid: $375

**20102** **George VI 5 Cents 1949,** KM42, Specimen 66 PCGS, Ex: Dominion. The current population data indicates that PCGS has certified 21 examples as Specimen 66 and just four finer Specimen 67 pieces (7/09). This amazing cameo Specimen exhibits fully prooflike fields around lustrous devices. Both sides have light gray surfaces and bold design motifs.
*From the Canadiana Collection*
Estimate: $350-$550   Starting Bid: $175

**20103** **George VI 5 Cents 1951 Nickel Bicentennial,** KM48, MS65 ICCS. Commemorating the bicentennial of the isolation of the metal nickel in 1751. This Gem has exceptional eye appeal that results from satiny light gray surfaces, bold design features, and a hint of cameo contrast on the reverse. PCGS has certified nine similar examples, with none finer (7/09).
*From the Canadiana Collection*
Estimate: $200-$400   No Minimum Bid

**20104** **George VI 5 Cents 1951 High Relief,** KM42a, MS67 PCGS, Ex: Lafortune. A brilliant prooflike representative, this chrome-steel piece has ice-blue surfaces. It is a Superb Gem coin with amazing eye appeal. These coins were struck in steel during the Korean War, when nickel was needed for the war effort. Few of the more than 4.3 million 1951 5 Cents pieces ended up as the High Relief variety. This example is the single finest Mint State coin that PCGS has certified (7/09).
*From the Canadiana Collection*
Estimate: $8,000-$10,000   Starting Bid: $4,000

**20103** **George VI 5 Cents 1951 Nickel Bicentennial,** KM48, MS65 ICCS. Commemorating the bicentennial of the isolation of the metal nickel in 1751. This Gem has exceptional eye appeal that results from satiny light gray surfaces, bold design features, and a hint of cameo contrast on the reverse. PCGS has certified nine similar examples, with none finer (7/09).
*From the Canadiana Collection*
Estimate: $200-$400   No Minimum Bid

**20105** **George VI 5 Cents 1952,** KM42a, MS66 PCGS, Ex: Pittman. Apparently from one of the 1952 sets offered in the first part of the Pittman sale, this boldly detailed beauty has satiny surfaces with reflective fields and lustrous devices. PCGS has certified two in MS66 and three finer coins (7/09).
*From the Canadiana Collection*
Estimate: $400-$600   Starting Bid: $200

**20106**  **Victoria 10 Cents 1858,** KM3, MS66 PCGS. An impeccably preserved 10 Cents Province issue, and an essential one-year type. The surfaces have acquired pleasing, natural gray and rose toning with iridescent flashes that emanate from the devices. The underlying mint luster is strong and flashes brightly through the multiple layers of toning. This is easily one of the finest 1858 10 Cents we have ever encountered, and a coin that is worthy of a runaway bid.
*From the Canadiana Collection*
Estimate: $6,500-$7,500  Starting Bid: $3,250

**20107**  **Victoria 10 Cents 1858 First 8/5,** KM3, AU58 PCGS, Ex: Dominion Collection. Undoubtedly struck from a single pair of dies, few examples are known in any grade. At the AU58 level, this is one of the finer pieces known of this curious overdate. The finest certified to date by PCGS is an MS63 (7/09). Significant amounts of mint luster remain on each side, and only slight evidence of handling is evident. The reverse is bright and semi-reflective, and each side has a light layer of golden-rose toning with a subtle accent of lilac on the Queen's face.
*From the Canadiana Collection*
Estimate: $8,000-$10,000  Starting Bid: $4,000

**20108** **Victoria 10 Cents 1870 Narrow 0,** KM3, MS65 PCGS. The Narrow 0 is the more available of the two date varieties. At the MS65 level, this coin is tied with two other pieces as the finest PCGS has certified (7/09). This is a deeply and originally toned example that has rich cobalt-blue and rose coloration intermingled over each side. The devices are sharply struck throughout. There are two prominent die cracks present—one on each side. The obverse crack connects the bottom hair curl to the back of the bust truncation; the reverse crack extends inward from the rim at 3 o'clock.
*From the Canadiana Collection*
Estimate: $6,500-$8,500   Starting Bid: $3,250

**20109** **Victoria 10 Cents 1870 Narrow 0,** KM3, Specimen 66 PCGS, Ex: Norweb. This is the finer of two Specimens that were offered in the famed Norweb holdings; the other was a Specimen 65 or MS65 piece—depending on whose opinion one took—that showed some slightly different die characteristics. Only a few dozen examples were produced in the Specimen sets of 1870. The Norweb catalog noted the repunching on the 10 in the denomination, the T in CENTS, and the 8 in the date. This coin today appears much as it did in the Norweb sale: "Indescribably beautiful electric blue and champagne toning against deep mirror surfaces on the obverse. The reverse is champagne and light magenta. A splendid coin in every respect." The PCGS holder specifies this piece as "reeded edge" (that service has certified one Specimen 50 coin with a plain edge, and Specimen coins of 1870 are known of other denominations with a plain edge). Here the edge is plainly visible through the PCGS encapsulation, revealing the edge reeding.
*From the Canadiana Collection*
Estimate: $8,000-$10,000   Starting Bid: $4,000

**20110** **Victoria 10 Cents 1870 Wide 0,** KM3, MS66 PCGS. Significantly scarcer than its Narrow 0 counterpart, the Wide 0 is also a condition rarity. Only six pieces have been certified in all Uncirculated grades—this is the finest (7/09). The fields show faint die striations that give each side slight semi-reflectivity with sharp definition on the devices. Both obverse and reverse are well-balanced with attractive rose-gray patina overall and bits of lilac interspersed. An important coin for the collector of early Dominion 10 Cents pieces.
*From the Canadiana Collection*
Estimate: $8,000-$10,000   Starting Bid: $4,000

**20111** **Victoria 10 Cents 1871,** KM3, MS66 PCGS. Considerably finer than the Belzberg and Pittman examples, and in fact the finest certified by PCGS (7/09). The issue apparently circulated widely, and few pieces were set aside in Uncirculated condition. This magnificently toned example boasts variegated crimson, gray, and emerald-green patina over each side, with bright underlying mint luster and a full strike throughout.
*From the Canadiana Collection*
Estimate: $7,500-$9,500   Starting Bid: $3,750

**20112**  **Victoria 10 Cents 1871-H, Reverse T1 7/7,** KM3, MS64 PCGS. The surfaces are thoroughly brilliant, and mint luster flashes across each side. The striking details are complete, with finely detailed hair on Victoria and full venation on the leaves. A few light abrasions keep this piece from the Gem category. This is the only MS64 example certified by PCGS, and only one coin is finer (7/09).
*From the Canadiana Collection*
Estimate: $2,500-$3,500   Starting Bid: $1,250

**20113**  **Victoria 10 Cents 1872-H,** KM3, MS64 PCGS. Surprisingly few examples are known today of the 1872-H despite a mintage of 1 million pieces. In all Mint State grades, PCGS has only certified eight pieces, with only two others in MS64 and none finer (7/09). This sharply impressed coin displays rich, original gray-russet toning over each side, with occasional flashes of lilac at the margins.
*From the Canadiana Collection*
Estimate: $6,500-$8,500   Starting Bid: $3,250

20114 **Victoria 10 Cents 1872-H,** KM3, Specimen 64 PCGS. A rarely seen example of an early Dominion 10 Cents. This piece is one of only seven examples certified by PCGS (7/09). As always, the reverse shows a number of shallow planchet flakes, seen here as brilliant areas that interrupt the toning. The obverse is brightly reflective, and the mirrors shine through the blue-green and rose patina. The reverse is not quite as reflective, with considerably deeper reddish-brown toning surrounded at the margins by deep blue toning. Identifiable by two tiny planchet flakes on the obverse: one in the center of Victoria's neck, and another along the jawline. This is the Charlton plate coin from the 63rd edition, page 402.
*From the Canadiana Collection*
Estimate: $3,500-$4,500   Starting Bid: $1,750

## Key 1875-H 10 Cents MS64—Tied for Finest Certified

20115 **Victoria 10 Cents 1875-H,** KM3, MS64 PCGS. A clerical error accounts for the uncertain number of 1874-H and 1875-H 10 Cents pieces, with both years' mintages combined being 1.6 million coins. The 1875-H is clearly the rarer of the two years and is considerably more valuable. Curiously, the number of coins submitted to PCGS is roughly the same for each year. However, it is obvious that the rarity of the 1875-H has driven a significant portion of the survivors to be certified, since 18 pieces have been graded in AG-VF conditions. Mint State pieces are legendary rarities with only seven examples certified in a tight cluster between MS62 and MS64 (none are in the MS60-MS61 range and none are finer than MS64). This piece is tied with three others at the MS64 level (7/09). The devices are sharply impressed on each side, and there are only minor luster grazes and tiny abrasions that keep the coin from an even higher grade. The surfaces are toned in rich shadings of deep gray, lilac, and rose. An outstanding opportunity for the specialist to acquire this key issue.
*From the Canadiana Collection*
Estimate: $40,000-$60,000 Starting Bid: $20,000

**20116** **Victoria 10 Cents 1880-H Obverse 2,** KM3, MS66 PCGS. Relatively available at most levels of Mint State, the 1880-H is not one of the glamour issues of this series. Even so, in this lofty condition, you have an opportunity to acquire one of only two pieces certified in MS66 by PCGS, with none finer (7/09). Well struck, with original rose-gray toning and full underlying luster.
*From the Canadiana Collection*
Estimate: $6,000-$6,500   Starting Bid: $3,000

**20117** **Victoria 10 Cents 1881-H,** KM3, MS66 PCGS. A rather scarce, lower population issue with only 12 total examples certified in Mints State by PCGS. This exemplary piece combines a near-flawless strike with lovely silver-gray and rose patina over pristine surfaces. One of only three certified in MS66 by PCGS, with none finer (7/09).
*From the Canadiana Collection*
Estimate: $7,500-$10,000   Starting Bid: $3,750

**20118** **Victoria 10 Cents 1882-H Obverse 3,** KM3, MS66 PCGS. With an Uncirculated population of 18 pieces, the 1882-H 10 Cents is one of the more available Heaton Mint issues. However, in MS66 it is a definite condition rarity as only one other piece has been so graded by PCGS, with one finer (7/09). The reverse shows especially strong striking definition in the intricately detailed leaf veins. The obverse has silver-gray centers with russet at the periphery, while the reverse displays uniform deep gray-russet toning. Both sides are highly lustrous.
*From the Canadiana Collection*
Estimate: $6,000-$8,000   Starting Bid: $3,000

**20119** **Victoria 10 Cents 1883-H,** KM3, MS66 PCGS. The second-rarest of the Heaton issues behind the 1875-H, although all the H-mint pieces in this series are elusive at the high Mint State levels. This MS66 example is tied for finest at PCGS with a single other example (7/09), and finer than the Belzberg (ex: Norweb) coin—a MS65. Original pinkish-gray toning on both sides blends with light blue at the rims creating a full complement of luster.
*From the Canadiana Collection*
Estimate: $8,000-$10,000   Starting Bid: $4,000

## Key 1884 Ten Cents—Single Finest Known

**20120  Victoria 10 Cents 1884,** KM3, MS65 PCGS. After a hiatus of 13 years, the Royal Mint once again struck 10 Cents pieces for Canada. The Royal Mint Report states 152,428 coins were produced from two obverse and two reverse die pairs, with a net mintage of 150,000 pieces. The Norweb catalog terms the date punch as "idiosyncratic," and indeed it is. Each digit appears to have been hand-punched into the die, and the numerals slant noticeably upward from left to right. Of the 51 pieces certified by PCGS of this issue, 43 are in circulated grades. The Norweb, Pittman, and Burhop coins were all in the VF-XF grade range. This is the single finest example certified by PCGS (7/09). The mint luster is bright and sparkles through the toning that covers each side. The surfaces are predominantly gray, with considerable amounts of blue interspersed over the reverse, while golden-lilac encircles the obverse rim. Very few marks are present, the only one worthy of mention is a diagonal abrasion just right of the N in CENTS. A remarkable opportunity to acquire this key Canadian rarity.
*From the Canadiana Collection*
Estimate: $35,000-$45,000  Starting Bid: $17,500

**20121  Victoria 10 Cents 1885 Obverse 4,** KM3, MS64 PCGS. We wrote in the Belzberg catalog (1/2003, lot 15306) that this issue was underrated, although prices have moved up sharply since then. This is still a fiendishly difficult issue. The present example is one of three near-Gems certified at PCGS (7/09), with only the Belzberg piece and two others finer—all MS65. Original pinkish-gold patina blends with powder-gray that outlines the rim lettering. Attractive and high-end, with a good strike and few signs of contact.
*From the Canadiana Collection*
Estimate: $8,000-$10,000   Starting Bid: $4,000

**20122  Victoria 10 Cents 1886 Small 6 Obverse 5,** KM3, MS64 PCGS. Three different styles of 6 were used on 1886 10 Cents pieces. The Small 6 is not an absolute rarity, but at the MS64 level this coin is among the finest obtainable, tied with two other PCGS coins (7/09). This is a lovely, high-end example that displays multicolored iridescent toning over each side and bright, sparkling mint luster. The strike is sharp, and just a couple of grade-limiting marks on Victoria's neck prevent an even higher grade.
*From the Canadiana Collection*
Estimate: $3,500-$5,000   Starting Bid: $1,750

**20123 Victoria 10 Cents 1886 Large Pointed 6 Obverse 5,** KM3, MS66 PCGS. This incredible coin is the finest of the Large Pointed 6 variety that PCGS has certified by eight grade points (an AU58 is second finest), and the sole Mint State example that PCGS has graded to date (7/09). We wrote in the Belzberg catalog that "we feel that the 1886 is one of the more underrated dimes in the 1880s and examples above XF are quite rare." This piece and its companions in the present sale are evidence of that statement. The margins have amber and gold predominating, melding into pinkish hues in the centers on both sides. There are no singular marks, as expected of the grade, with top-shelf eye appeal.
*From the Canadiana Collection*
Estimate: $15,000-$20,000   Starting Bid: $7,500

**20124 Victoria 10 Cents 1886 Large Knob 6 Obverse 5,** KM3, MS65 PCGS. This beautiful Gem example is the sole finest of this elusive issue certified at PCGS, which has seen only four Mint State pieces (7/09). Both sides show splendid eye appeal, with pinkish-gold patina blending into ice-blue at the rim. The bold strike and paucity of contact further increase the obvious allure.
*From the Canadiana Collection*
Estimate: $10,000-$12,000   Starting Bid: $5,000

**20125  Victoria 10 Cents 1887,** KM3, MS64 PCGS. The 1887 is a scarce and underrated 10 Cents issue. The mintage was a net 350,000 pieces out of a total struck of 377,644. It is not difficult to imagine how few examples were saved in 19th century Canada, and indeed the 1887 is a significant absolute as well as condition rarity today. PCGS has certified only 27 coins of this date in all grades, and a mere 10 pieces have been graded in mint condition. This piece is tied with three others as the finest graded by PCGS (7/09). The mint luster is especially pronounced and frosted on each side. The obverse is mostly untoned in the center with rose-gold accents around the margin, while the reverse has the same colors but more evenly distributed. The devices are sharply struck throughout, and there are no singularly noticeable abrasions.
*From the Canadiana Collection*
Estimate: $5,500-$7,500  Starting Bid: $2,750

**20126  Victoria 10 Cents 1888,** KM3, MS65 PCGS. With a mintage of half a million pieces one might expect the 1888 to be more available than it is. PCGS has only certified 29 pieces in all grades (7/09). Surprisingly, 20 of those coins are in various Uncirculated grades, which would indicate the existence of a small hoard (roll?) at one time. This example is tied with two others at the MS65 level, the finest certified. The mint luster is softly frosted, and except for a hint of golden peripheral color, the coin is untoned. The devices on each side are well brought up, with just a few tiny, pinprick field marks on both sides.
*From the Canadiana Collection*
Estimate: $3,500-$4,500  Starting Bid: $1,750

## Exceptional MS66 1889 Ten Cents

20127 **Victoria 10 Cents 1889,** KM3, MS66 PCGS. The mintage for the 1889 10 Cents was an unimpressive 600,000 pieces. However, it is generally thought that most of those coins were actually dated 1888. The realization of the rarity and value of this date is an interesting one. As related in the Norweb catalog, the *Canadian Antiquarian* issue of January 1890 commented:

"Specimens of the coinage of 1889 are still scarce in this vicinity (Montreal) indicating that it must have been issued from some of the distant offices of the receiver-general."

In 1950, Leslie C. Hill could only account for 16 pieces. That was also the last year an 1889 10 Cents was found in circulation. The rarity of the date was generally unrecognized just three years earlier with the *Charlton Catalogue* from 1947 only valuing the date at $1.25 in Uncirculated. However, John Pittman paid $67 for the Mint State coin he purchased in 1951. Just 13 years later, in 1964, an Uncirculated 1889 brought $3,300 in the CNA Sale.

While exact mintage figures are impossible to determine, the best guess today is that somewhere between 10,000 and 20,000 pieces were actually struck with the 1889 date. Undoubtedly, this mintage was accomplished with one die pairing. The diagnostic die crack at the left side of the second I in VICTORIA is faintly seen here. The diagnostic tiny dot to the left of the final A in CANADA is also light. We do not see the raised curved line that extends from the upper space of that same A, suggesting this piece was struck from an early die state.

This is far and away the finest 1889 10 Cents certified by PCGS (7/09). The next finest grade is MS63, represented by two pieces. The surfaces on this example are nearly flawless. Both obverse and reverse are evenly balanced, with lovely gray-lilac toning. The reverse displays considerable reflectivity, a feature that is absent in the obverse fields. The devices are sharply detailed throughout. This is an opportunity for the advanced collector to acquire what is unquestionably the finest example of the rarest date in the Canadian 10 Cents series.
*From the Canadiana Collection*
Estimate: $80,000-$100,000  Starting Bid: $40,000

**20128 Victoria 10 Cents 1890H,** KM3, MS66 PCGS. Only 450,000 pieces were struck of the 1890H, and to date (7/09) a mere 17 coins have been certified in all grades at PCGS. Of those, 10 pieces are in Mint State, and this coin is tied with two others as the finest certified. This piece shows the usually seen die crack from the 0 in the denomination through the N in CENTS, continuing to the lower rim. This piece is finer than the Belzberg, Norweb, and Pittman examples of this so-called "common" date. The surfaces show thick mint frost, and each side has light gray-brilliance surrounded by golden and teal coloration. Each side is sharply struck, with no noticeable abrasions.
*From the Canadiana Collection*
Estimate: $4,000-$6,000 Starting Bid: $2,000

**20129 Victoria 10 Cents 1891 21 Leaves,** KM3, MS66 PCGS. The 1891 10 Cents offers a significant and highly collectible variant based upon the use of the old or new reverse hub. The present coin was struck from the old reverse hub, which was used from 1870-1881 and again in 1891. Such pieces show 21 leaves in the wreath, rather than the 22 leaves seen on all other 10 Cents beginning in 1882. Of the 10 pieces certified in all Uncirculated grades, this piece is tied with one other as finest certified by PCGS (7/09). Close examination reveals faint die striations in the fields on each side, which give the coin a bright, semi-prooflike appearance. This is notable even through the multiple layers of sea-green and rose toning that cover each side. Slight softness is seen at the top of Victoria's hair; the reverse is completely brought up.
*From the Canadiana Collection*
Estimate: $6,500-$8,500 Starting Bid: $3,250

20130  **Victoria 10 Cents 1891 22 Leaves,** KM3, MS66 PCGS, Ex: Dominion. Deep intermingled iridescent toning creates extraordinary eye appeal on this fully original 10 Cents. This is the Dominion Collection example, although it has been regraded since then and probably accounts for both MS66 examples appearing on the *PCGS Population Report.* None have been certified finer. The 22 Leaves is more plentiful than the 21 Leaves, but neither is easy to find—especially in higher grades. The Belzberg Collection had a MS64, the Norweb Collection an AU58. We believe the present piece is the finest known example (7/09).
*From the Canadiana Collection*
Estimate: $6,500-$8,500   Starting Bid: $3,250

20131  **Victoria 10 Cents 1892 Small 9 Obverse 5,** KM3, MS66 PCGS. This is an important rarity, unpriced above XF in the *Charlton Standard Catalogue.* PCGS has certified two submissions in MS66, the finest at that service (7/09). The Belzberg and Dominion collections each had a MS63, while the Norweb Collection had an AU50. Now consider the present piece in MS66, a coin that will appeal to the specialist. This lovely Premium Gem has medium-gray toning with sunset-orange peripheral toning on the obverse. The reverse has amber, lilac, and sea-green toning. Both sides have reflective fields that increase the amazing eye appeal.
*From the Canadiana Collection*
Estimate: $10,000-$12,000   Starting Bid: $5,000

**20132   Victoria 10 Cents 1892/1 Large 9 Obverse 6,** KM3, MS62 PCGS. This extremely important overdate variety was an 1891 Large 9 die that was repunched with a 2 over the 1. Aside from the large 9, the base of the 1 is visible beneath the right side of the base of the 2. The portrait is defined as T6 in the *Charlton Standard Catalogue.* The overdate variety is a major rarity in the early 10 Cents series. PCGS has only certified five pieces in all grades, and the present example is the only Mint State coin (7/09). It is sharply detailed with brilliant silver luster, entirely devoid of toning. The Dominion Collection had an AU55; the Belzberg Collection lacked this variety. The Norweb coin was a MS60.
*From the Canadiana Collection*
Estimate: $7,500-$10,000   Starting Bid: $3,750

**20133   Victoria 10 Cents 1893 Flat Top 3,** KM3, MS67 PCGS. With 1893 10 Cents coins, the choice is between rare and rarer. The Round Top 3 is definitely the rarer of the two variants, as well as one of the keys to the Canadian series. But the Flat Top 3 is an overlooked issue. The net mintage was recorded as 500,000 pieces, and that number was achieved using 10 obverse dies and nine reverse dies. Obviously attrition took a heavy toll. To date (7/09), PCGS has certified 29 pieces ranging from VG to MS67, including the present coin which is the sole finest certified. One die pair of Flat Top 3 dimes shows light repunching on the 18 in the date and dramatic repunching on the 9; this was noted on both the Norweb and Pittman coins. This particular piece is obviously from a different die pair, as it shows no trace of such repunching.

The Flat Top 1893 10 Cents is an issue that would be valued even more highly if it were not in the shadows of the Round Top 3. We estimate that 100-120 pieces are known of both varieties combined, of which the Flat Top 3 comprises of perhaps two-thirds of the population, and the Round Top 3 one-third. If there are only twice as many Flat Top 3s as Round Tops, then the Flat Top is truly underrated—the Round Top coins are 10 times more expensive in Mint State, and even more so in circulated grades.

The surfaces on this finest-certified piece are clearly original. Each side shows areas of interspersed brilliance and russet toning. The striking details are strong throughout, with full definition on the reverse leaves. Two tiny, near-undetectable marks serve as pedigree identifiers, both are located at the top of the hair below the TI in GRATIA.
*From the Canadiana Collection*
Estimate: $15,000-$20,000   Starting Bid: $7,500

**20134 Victoria 10 Cents 1893 Round Top 3,** KM3, AU55 PCGS. The Round Top 3 is the most highly recognized issue in the entire Canadian 10 Cents series. It is also a transcendent rarity that is widely recognized by non-Canadian collectors. Estimates vary about the numbers struck and the number that survive. The estimate in the Norweb Collection was 100-200 pieces. In the Pittman Sale catalog, Akers stated estimates range from a low of 25 pieces to a high of 100 coins. The KM reference gives a definitive "92 pcs. known", but the actual number is probably no more than 50 coins. PCGS has graded 32 examples, and the finest is a MS64. At the AU55 level, only one other piece has been so graded, with two finer (7/09).

Only slight evidence of friction is apparent on each side, and the only mentionable mark is a tiny diagonal mark above the E in CENTS. The surfaces are light gray over the design high points and the obverse center, with deep gray patina around the obverse periphery and reverse devices. Sharply struck throughout.
*From the Canadiana Collection*
Estimate: $7,500-$10,000   Starting Bid: $3,750

**20135 Victoria 10 Cents 1894 Obverse 6,** KM3, MS65 PCGS. Light gray and pale green obverse toning and deep steel reverse hues point to the originality of this Gem. The design motifs are boldly executed. It is the only MS65 that PCGS has certified, with just one finer MS66 (7/09). This is another conditional rarity among 19th century Canadian coins. The Dominion Collection had a MS64, while the Belzberg and Norweb collections each had a MS63. An exceptional opportunity for the specialist.
*From the Canadiana Collection*
Estimate: $5,000-$7,000   Starting Bid: $2,500

**20136 Victoria 10 Cents 1896 Obverse 6,** KM3, MS66 PCGS. This amazing Premium Gem exhibits bold design details with fully brilliant and frosty silver surfaces that are essentially untoned, aside from wispy champagne highlights. One of three pieces that PCGS has certified as MS66, with none finer (7/09). It is finer than the Dominion and Belzberg MS64 coins, and far above the Norweb AU55 example. The finest we have ever handled.
*From the Canadiana Collection*
Estimate: $4,000-$6,000  Starting Bid: $2,000

**20137 Victoria 10 Cents 1898 Obverse 6,** KM3, MS66 PCGS. This Premium Gem is one of three PCGS-certified MS66 examples, with none finer (7/09). It is equal to the Belzberg coin and finer than the MS65 Dominion Collection example or the Norweb MS64. This fully original piece has medium gray surfaces and gorgeous iridescent toning over frosty luster. All design elements are sharply impressed.
*From the Canadiana Collection*
Estimate: $5,000-$7,000  Starting Bid: $2,500

**20138** **Victoria 10 Cents 1899 Small 9s,** KM3, MS66 PCGS, Ex: Cornwell-Campbell. The more available of the two differing date styles for the year, but still quite elusive in the top Mint State grades. This Premium Gem is one of three MS66s at PCGS, with a single MS67 finer—the Belzberg (ex: Norweb) coin (7/09). Predominantly pinkish-gray with accents of violet, indigo, and teal near the rims, a well-struck and eye-appealing coin. Note that the 899 digits are much more deeply impressed into the die than the 1 at the beginning of the date. From a mintage of 1.2 million pieces—including both varieties.
*From the Canadiana Collection*
Estimate: $6,500-$8,500   Starting Bid: $3,250

**20139** **Victoria 10 Cents 1899 Large 9s,** KM3, MS65 PCGS. The 1899 Large 9s dime is significantly scarcer than its Small 9s counterpart. In Mint State, the Large 9s is about twice as rare. Splashes of violet, blue-green, gold, and silver-gray colors drape the surfaces of this lustrous Gem. The strike is nearly full, with a couple of pin-sized handling marks. An appealing example of this elusive issue. PCGS Population: four in 65, one finer (7/09).
*From the Canadiana Collection*
Estimate: $6,500-$8,500   Starting Bid: $3,250

**20140** **Victoria 10 Cents 1900,** KM3, MS66 PCGS. Mottled purple, blue, and silver-gray toning covers both sides of this sharply struck Premium Gem. Shimmering satiny luster enhances the eye appeal. The surfaces appear perfect to the unaided eye, and a loupe locates only a couple of minuscule abrasions. A great condition rarity. PCGS has certified only four MS66 examples, and none are finer (7/09).
*From the Canadiana Collection*
Estimate: $2,000-$3,000   Starting Bid: $1,000

**20141** **Victoria 10 Cents 1901,** KM3, MS67 PCGS. An outstanding, conditionally rare piece. This is the finest example by two grade points certified by PCGS, with the next finest coins graded MS65 (7/09). The 1901 was the final year of Victoria's reign, and the present coin would make a fantastic representative. Appealing light-green, lavender, and gold toning envelops both sides of this carefully preserved Superb Gem. A few minuscule handling marks blend well with the lovely patina. Magnificent satiny luster shines throughout the surfaces. The design elements are powerfully impressed.
*From the Canadiana Collection*
Estimate: $5,000-$7,000   Starting Bid: $2,500

**20142** **Edward VII 10 Cents 1902,** KM10, MS65 PCGS. A popular first-year issue with a mintage well below the impressive 1 million-coin mark. Deep blue and violet toning around the margins contrasts against gold and silver-gray centers. Eye-catching luster fills the fields. The strike is razor-sharp, and there are only a few wispy luster grazes. PCGS has certified just four MS65 examples, with none finer (7/09).
*From the Canadiana Collection*
Estimate: $2,500-$3,500   Starting Bid: $1,250

**20143** **Edward VII 10 Cents 1902-H,** KM10, MS67 PCGS. The 1902-H is one of the most available Edward VII dimes in middle Mint State grades. Above MS65, however, it becomes rare, and this piece is the only MS67 example graded by PCGS, with none finer (7/09). This wondrous representative exhibits eye-catching satiny luster and a full strike. Inspection reveals only a couple of tiny handling marks. A hint of rose and yellow toning in the periphery enhances mostly silver-gray surfaces.
*From the Canadiana Collection*
Estimate: $2,500-$3,500   Starting Bid: $1,250

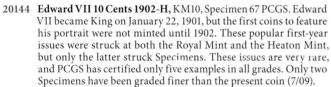

**20144  Edward VII 10 Cents 1902-H,** KM10, Specimen 67 PCGS. Edward VII became King on January 22, 1901, but the first coins to feature his portrait were not minted until 1902. These popular first-year issues were struck at both the Royal Mint and the Heaton Mint, but only the latter struck Specimens. These issues are very rare, and PCGS has certified only five examples in all grades. Only two Specimens have been graded finer than the present coin (7/09).

Delicate gold toning accents the margins, while the centers are pale gray. A number of die polish lines are seen in the fields, and there is impressive luster throughout. Both sides appear pristine to the unaided eye. A sharply struck and appealing Superb Gem.
*From the Canadiana Collection*
Estimate: $12,000-$15,000  Starting Bid: $6,000

**20145  Edward VII 10 Cents 1903,** KM10, MS66 PCGS. The 1903 10 Cents is the key to the Edward VII series, with a low mintage of just 500,000 pieces. Circulated examples are available, but they command a significant premium. Only a few Mint State pieces exist, and they are seldom offered for sale by their proud owners. As one can imagine, the 1903 is quite significant in MS66. This piece is tied with one other at PCGS as the finest certified. The next highest examples are two points below (7/09).

Variegated gold, purple, red, and steel-blue toning envelops the satiny surfaces. Close examination with a loupe reveals only a few insignificant marks. The strike is a touch soft on Edward's crown, but the rest of the details are boldly impressed. This appealing Premium Gem represents an important opportunity for the advanced collector.
*From the Canadiana Collection*
Estimate: $8,000-$10,000  Starting Bid: $4,000

**20146** **Edward VII 10 Cents 1903-H,** KM10, MS67 PCGS. The Birmingham Mint issues, designated by the letter H, are generally better struck and more available than their Royal Mint counterparts. The present coin, however, is a cut above the rest—the finest example certified by PCGS (7/09). This delightfully toned Superb Gem exhibits a mix of light-green, violet, red, yellow-gold, and silver-gray. The surfaces appear nearly pristine to the unaided eye, and the strike is razor-sharp. Wonderful satiny luster enhances the eye appeal.
*From the Canadiana Collection*
Estimate: $4,500-$6,500   Starting Bid: $2,250

**20147** **Edward VII 10 Cents 1904,** KM10, MS66 PCGS. The 1904 dime in the Norweb Collection was graded AU58 and the cataloger noted that it is "quite elusive in Mint State, and the Norwebs were not able to find one." PCGS has graded just 21 examples in Mint State, of which the present coin is the single finest (7/09).

Pleasing shades of blue, green, purple, and red intermingle on both sides of this attractive Premium Gem. Flashy luster fills the fields and highlights the powerfully struck design elements. Inspection with a loupe reveals only a few inconsequential handling marks. This conditionally rare piece belongs in an important collection of Canadian coins.
*From the Canadiana Collection*
Estimate: $3,500-$5,000   Starting Bid: $1,750

**20148  Edward VII 10 Cents 1905,** KM10, MS66 PCGS. One of the more challenging Edward VII issues in high grades, the 1905 is rarely seen above Select Mint State. PCGS has graded four pieces in MS64, one in MS65, and just the present coin—the finest example certified—in MS66 (7/09).

Delightful violet patina encircles the golden-brown and silver-gray center of the obverse, while the reverse has a more random mix of lilac and hazel toning. Dazzling satiny luster radiates beneath the attractive patina. The strike is nearly full, and there are only a few tiny grazes on each side. A magnificent representative.
*From the Canadiana Collection*
Estimate: $5,000-$7,000   Starting Bid: $2,500

**20149  Edward VII 10 Cents 1906,** KM10, MS65 PCGS. The 1906 10 Cents ranks in the middle of the Edward VII series in terms of rarity. Only a select few examples have survived in high grades. The present coin is lightly toned with wafts of tan, yellow-gold, and blue. Several minuscule marks do not distract. Glistening satiny luster abounds in the fields and highlights the powerfully struck design elements. PCGS Population: three in 65, two finer (7/09).
*From the Canadiana Collection*
Estimate: $2,000-$3,000   Starting Bid: $1,000

**20150 Edward VII 10 Cents 1907,** KM10, MS67 PCGS. Mottled sky-blue, violet, red-orange, and silver-gray toning coats the highly lustrous surfaces. The crown on the obverse is a trifle soft, but the rest of the details are exquisite. Both sides appear virtually immaculate, with only a couple of wispy grazes visible under magnification. The 1907 is conditionally rare in high grades. This Superb Gem is the finest example graded at PCGS by two points (7/09).
*From the Canadiana Collection*
Estimate: $3,000-$5,000  Starting Bid: $1,500

**20151 Edward VII 10 Cents 1908,** KM10, MS65 PCGS. A touch of light brown patina accents the mostly silver-gray obverse, which contrasts against vibrant purple and blue toning on the reverse margins. Numerous die polish lines are visible in the reverse fields, but there are no significant marks. The strike is sharp, save for a touch of softness on Edward's hair. Flashy luster enhances the appeal.
*From the Canadiana Collection*
Estimate: $1,750-$2,250  Starting Bid: $875

**20152 Edward VII 10 Cents 1909 Victorian Leaves,** KM10, MS64 PCGS. We don't really understand what PCGS means by "Large Leaves," as the Victorian Leaves variety clearly has the smaller leaves of the two 1909 varieties. The *Charlton Catalogue* refers to this reverse design as "Victorian Leaves." Lovely purple toning drapes both sides of this well-defined near-Gem. The surfaces appear remarkably clean for the grade, with only a couple insignificant abrasions. Flashy luster adds to the aesthetic appeal. PCGS Population: 3 in 64, 1 finer (7/09).
*From the Canadiana Collection*
Estimate: $1,500-$2,000  Starting Bid: $750

**20154** **Edward VII 10 Cents 1910,** KM10, MS65 ICCS. Delicate yellow toning near the rims adds color to this essentially brilliant Gem. A few minuscule abrasions do not affect the overall outstanding eye appeal. Powerful luster highlights the razor-sharp design elements. An excellent example of the final issue under Edward VII. The 1910 is virtually impossible to locate in a higher grade.
*From the Canadiana Collection*
Estimate: $1,000-$1,300   Starting Bid: $500

**20155** **George V 10 Cents 1911,** KM17, MS67 PCGS. This is the important one-year variety with the "Godless" obverse. When a new obverse was created for George V, the customary DEI GRATIA (by the grace of God), or abbreviation thereof, was omitted, prompting public criticism. The following year a new obverse was prepared with the restored legend. Rings of lime-green, teal, cobalt-blue, and red surround both sides of this nearly pristine Superb Gem. A resplendent and boldly struck example. PCGS Population: 7 in 67, 0 finer (7/09).
*From the Canadiana Collection*
Estimate: $1,200-$1,500   Starting Bid: $600

**20153** **Edward VII 10 Cents 1909 Broad Leaves,** KM10, MS65 PCGS. In 1909, a new reverse was prepared for the dime that featured wide leaves with pronounced veins. Both the older Victorian and the new Broad Leaves reverses were used during that year. Although the exact mintage of each type is unknown (the combined emission was just under 1.7 million coins) the Broad Leaves reverse is undoubtedly scarcer—especially in Mint State. Splendid reddish-purple patina enhances the satiny surfaces of this razor-sharp Gem. A few minuscule marks blend well with the vibrant patina. PCGS has certified only one example finer (7/09).
*From the Canadiana Collection*
Estimate: $3,500-$5,000   Starting Bid: $1,750

**20156** **George V 10 Cents 1912,** KM23, MS66 PCGS. Purple and reddish-gold patina encircles the bright silver-gray centers. Several pin-sized abrasions keep this piece from the MS67 level. Dazzling satiny luster shimmers throughout the fields. The details are exquisite. PCGS has certified just six pieces in MS66, with none finer (7/09).
*From the Canadiana Collection*
Estimate: $3,000-$4,000  Starting Bid: $1,500

**20157** **George V 10 Cents 1913 Small Leaves,** KM23, MS66 PCGS, Ex: Belzberg. In the Belzberg catalog, we succinctly described this coin as: "Sharply defined with golden toned surfaces. No coins have been graded finer by PCGS." As of this writing (7/09), PCGS has still not certified a better example after six years. This lustrous Premium Gem has excellent eye appeal and would certainly please the connoisseur.
*From the Canadiana Collection*
Estimate: $1,500-$2,000  Starting Bid: $750

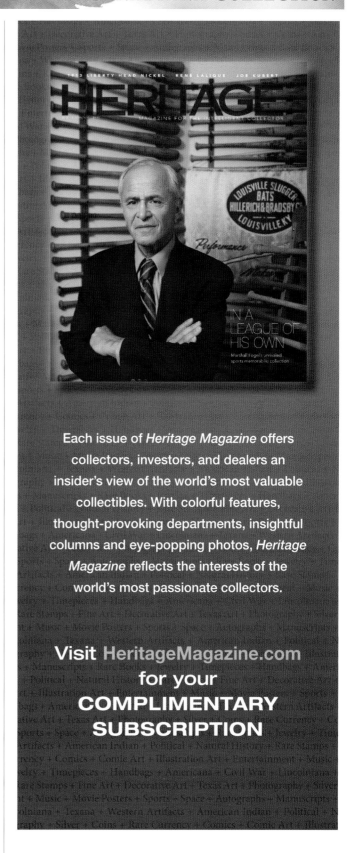

## Beautiful Broad Leaves 10 Cents 1913—Tied for Finest Certified by PCGS

20158   **George V 10 Cents 1913 Broad Leaves,** KM23, MS64 PCGS. The Broad Leaves hub was introduced in 1909, but used intermittently through 1913. The 1913 10 Cents is certainly not a rare date, with 3.6 million pieces produced. However, one die was used from a previous year with the old Broad Leaves reverse on only a slim portion of the pieces. Not only did this die receive limited use, but the 1913 Broad Leaves is one of the great condition rarities among all Canadian 10 Cents issue. PCGS has certified only four Mint State pieces, of which this coin is tied for finest (7/09). To give an idea of the rarity of this issue in Uncirculated grades, the Norweb Broad Leaves was a VF20, the Pittman example was Choice AU, and the Belzberg coin was an MS62.

The surfaces are generally untoned in the centers, with a light accent of reddish-gold around the margins. The luster is satiny and interrupted by only the smallest abrasions, which are mostly unnoticeable without a loupe. Only the Specimen 1936 Dot 10 Cents is rarer than the 1913 Broad Leaves. This is a rare opportunity for the Canadian collector and an especially important coin in this condition.
*From the Canadiana Collection*
Estimate: $25,000-$35,000  Starting Bid: $12,500

20159 **George V 10 Cents 1914,** KM23, MS66 PCGS. Charming shades of red, gold, purple, and green intermingle on the well-preserved surfaces of this satiny Premium Gem. The strike is nearly full, and both sides appear remarkably clean, even under magnification. An attractive representative. Only one example (a MS67) has been graded finer by PCGS (7/09).
*From the Canadiana Collection*
Estimate: $1,500-$2,000   Starting Bid: $750

20161 **George V 10 Cents 1916,** KM23, MS67 PCGS. Lovely rose-gold, lilac, steel-blue, and light green patina enhances the surfaces of this powerfully impressed Superb Gem. Several delicate die cracks are visible on each side. A couple of nearly imperceptible handling marks preclude perfection. Captivating satiny luster enhances the outstanding eye appeal. PCGS has certified only five pieces at the MS67 level, with none finer (7/09).
*From the Canadiana Collection*
Estimate: $2,500-$3,500   Starting Bid: $1,250

20160 **George V 10 Cents 1915,** KM23, MS67 PCGS. The 1915 10 Cents had a relatively low mintage of 688,057 coins—a significant drop from the previous year's emission of over 2.5 million pieces. Hazel and maroon grace the obverse perimeter, while the centers are silver-gray. The reverse is brilliant, save for a touch of toning near the border. Captivating satiny luster glistens across the virtually perfect surfaces. A powerfully struck and appealing example. PCGS has certified only two pieces in MS67, with none finer (7/09).
*From the Canadiana Collection*
Estimate: $5,000-$7,000   Starting Bid: $2,500

20162 **George V 10 Cents 1917,** KM23, MS67 PCGS. Splashes of teal, cobalt-blue, and red accent the obverse rim, while the center is bright silver-gray. The reverse is nearly brilliant, with a touch of gold and purple near the border. Appealing satiny luster highlights needle-sharp design elements, and no marks are visible to the unaided eye. Although available in most grades, the 1917 is rare in MS67. PCGS reports just two such examples, with one finer (7/09).
*From the Canadiana Collection*
Estimate: $2,000-$3,000   Starting Bid: $1,000

20163 **George V 10 Cents 1918,** KM23, MS68 PCGS. The 1918 had a substantial mintage due to increased demands from the wartime economy. Examples are easily available in almost all grades, but at the MS68 level this issue is an incredible rarity. Amazingly, only three Canadian 10 Cents struck before the year 2000 have been certified at that remarkable level. The present coin is the finest 1918 dime graded by PCGS (7/09).

This memorable example boasts spectacular semi-prooflike reflectivity beneath attractive toning. A medley of lilac, gold, hazel, and silver-gray drapes both sides. The strike is full, and the surfaces appear flawless to the unaided eye. This piece would be a highlight of any collection.
*From the Canadiana Collection*
Estimate: $6,500-$8,500   Starting Bid: $3,250

**20164** **George V 10 Cents 1919,** KM23, MS67 PCGS. Spectacular satiny luster shines throughout virtually perfect surfaces. Mottled violet, light green, deep red, and gold toning drapes both sides. The strike is full. The 1919 is one of the most available George V 10 Cents, and this piece makes a fantastic representative. PCGS has certified only two MS67 coins, with none finer (7/09).
*From the Canadiana Collection*
Estimate: $1,750-$2,250   Starting Bid: $875

**20166** **George V 10 Cents 1921,** KM23a, MS67 PCGS. Wafts of violet, gold, and medium-brown complement the predominantly silver-gray surfaces. Numerous striations are visible on the reverse, but both sides are nearly devoid of any marks. Delightful satiny luster shimmers across the surfaces. This precisely struck piece boasts tremendous eye appeal and is tied with one other coin for the finest certified by PCGS (7/09).
*From the Canadiana Collection*
Estimate: $2,000-$3,000   Starting Bid: $1,000

**20165** **George V 10 Cents 1920,** KM23a, MS67 PCGS. The last year that Canadian coins were struck with a sterling fineness (.925 silver) was in 1919, and in 1920 the composition was changed to 80% silver, 20% copper. Splendid reddish-gold and violet toning covers both sides of this virtually immaculate Superb Gem. A loupe locates only a couple of pin-sized marks. Coruscating satiny luster complements the boldly struck design elements. This is the only coin graded MS67 by PCGS, with none finer (7/09). An outstanding piece worthy of an important collection.
*From the Canadiana Collection*
Estimate: $2,000-$3,000   Starting Bid: $1,000

**20167** **George V 10 Cents 1928,** KM23a, MS67 PCGS. After a seven-year hiatus, coinage of 10 Cents pieces resumed with the 1928. An attractive medley of gold, purple, light green, and rose-red covers both sides of this carefully preserved Superb Gem. Scintillating satiny luster highlights the exquisitely defined details. PCGS Population: 2 in 67, 0 finer (7/09).
*From the Canadiana Collection*
Estimate: $2,500-$3,500 Starting Bid: $1,250

**20168** **George V 10 Cents 1929,** KM23a, MS66 PCGS, Ex: Belzberg. Lovely golden-brown accents grace the obverse, which contrasts nicely against the red and gold reverse. The satiny surfaces are free from any disturbances, and the eye appeal is superior. A fully struck Premium Gem. PCGS has certified only one example finer (7/09).
*From the Canadiana Collection*
Estimate: $500-$800 Starting Bid: $250

**20169** **George V 10 Cents 1930,** KM23a, MS67 PCGS. Mintage decreases significantly after the 1929 dime, and consequently the 1930 is about twice as scarce in high grades. Outstanding luster shimmers throughout the lightly toned surfaces. Splendid rosy accents grace the periphery. The strike is razor-sharp, and only a couple of wispy grazes are visible under magnification. An excellent representative. PCGS has certified only two MS67 coins, with none finer (7/09).
*From the Canadiana Collection*
Estimate: $2,500-$3,500 Starting Bid: $1,250

**20170** **George V 10 Cents 1931,** KM23a, MS66 PCGS. Deep red and purple toning fills the margins, with the occasional yellow-gold accent. Both sides appear pristine to the unaided eye, and only a few tiny abrasions are seen under magnification. The design elements exhibit strong detail, and the fields show impressive luster. A fantastic representative of the issue. PCGS has certified just one piece (a MS67) finer (7/09).
*From the Canadiana Collection*
Estimate: $500-$800 Starting Bid: $250

**20171 George V 10 Cents 1932,** KM23a, MS67 PCGS. Vibrant cobalt-blue, violet, and golden-brown toning surrounds silver-gray centers. Impressive satiny luster glistens throughout. Several virtually microscopic marks keep this needle-sharp piece from being absolutely flawless. This outstanding representative would please even the most discerning eye. PCGS has certified only two examples in MS67 and none finer (7/09).
*From the Canadiana Collection*
Estimate: $2,500-$3,500   Starting Bid: $1,250

**20172 George V 10 Cents 1933,** KM23a, MS66 PCGS. This attractively toned Premium Gem features intermingled blue, light green, magenta, rose, and gold. Flashy luster highlights the exquisitely defined design elements. A few minuscule handling marks blend nicely with the deep patina. The 1933 becomes elusive in the upper Mint State grades. PCGS reports just one finer example (7/09).
*From the Canadiana Collection*
Estimate: $1,500-$1,800   Starting Bid: $750

**20173 George V 10 Cents 1934,** KM23a, MS67 PCGS. Production of 10 Cents steadily declined after the large mintages during World War I. The 1934 issue was a diminutive 409,067 coins—the lowest yearly output since 1887. Interest in Canadian numismatics increased slightly around this time, but many people still did not collect by date. Mint State examples are scarce.

A touch of light red-orange patina complements mostly brilliant surfaces. Shimmering satiny luster enhances the eye appeal. Several pin-sized abrasions are nearly imperceptible without a loupe. The strike is razor-sharp. PCGS has certified two pieces at the MS67 level, with none finer (7/09).
*From the Canadiana Collection*
Estimate: $4,500-$6,500   Starting Bid: $2,250

20174 **George V 10 Cents 1935,** KM23a, MS67 PCGS. This outstanding Superb Gem boasts captivating satiny luster and powerfully impressed details. Delightful gold and lilac toning in the margins yields to silver-gray in the centers. A couple of tiny grazes are nearly imperceptible to the unaided eye. The 1935 had the lowest reported mintage of any George V 10 Cents at 384,056 pieces, although the 1913 Broad Leaves variety comprised only a small portion of that year's emission. This is the finest example certified by PCGS (7/09).
*From the Canadiana Collection*
Estimate: $3,500-$4,500   Starting Bid: $1,750

20175 **George V 10 Cents 1936,** KM23a, MS67 PCGS. Although plentiful in most grades, the 1936 is difficult to locate in this lofty level of preservation. PCGS has graded only seven MS67 pieces (7/09). A ring of red-orange and pale blue patina fills the obverse periphery, while the center is light gray. The reverse, in contrast, exhibits a more random mix of toning, and the margins are particularly colorful. The strike is bold, and there are only a few pin-sized abrasions. The final 10 Cents issued under the reign of George V.
*From the Canadiana Collection*
Estimate: $2,500-$3,500   Starting Bid: $1,250

## Heralded 1936 Dot 10 Cents Specimen 68 *Ex Pittman*

**20176** **George V 10 Cents 1936 Dot,** KM23a, Specimen 68 PCGS. With our offering of this example, Heritage will have brought to auction all three examples of the 1936 Dot 10 Cents that exist outside of museum collections. As a Specimen 68, this piece is five grade points finer than the Dominion Collection Specimen offered in September 2006 and two points finer than the Pittman-Belzberg Specimen sold in January 2003. The three Specimens are easily distinguished; while the Dominion example has rich gold and charcoal toning and the Pittman-Belzberg coin has deep and colorful blue-violet toning, this piece, which was lacquered, is generally light silver-gray with a touch of gold over the centers and small areas of deeper color at the D of IND in the obverse legend and just off the C of CANADA on the reverse. The texture of the fields has variously been called matte or satiny—due to the amount of swirling luster present on this piece, this cataloger prefers the latter term. Semantics aside, the surfaces are virtually perfect, and the definition is exquisite, particularly on the fine details of the portrait's hair and robes.

As David Akers noted in 1997 when he described this Specimen for the John Jay Pittman Collection, Part One, "no 1936 Dot 10 Cent piece has ever been offered for sale at public auction until this example offered here." In this way, the 1936 Dot 10 Cents was a private rarity of Pittman's, in contrast to the 1936 Dot Cent, which had received substantially more collector-publication ink and had made an appearance at public auction in 1961. (The Dominion Collection example became known to collectors after his passing.) At each auction appearance, the 1936 Dot 10 Cents has attracted plenty of attention and highly competitive bidding, and the offering of the finest survivor known is sure to increase the stakes.

*Ex: Maurice LaFortune, employee of the Royal Canadian Mint; John Jay Pittman, purchased 11/12/1951 as part of a complete 1936 Dot Specimen set, $400; unknown thieves, 1964, later returned anonymously along with the 1936 Dot Cent; John Jay Pittman Collection, Part One (David Akers, 10/1997), lot 15, $132,000. From the Canadiana Collection*
Estimate: $175,000-$225,000  Starting Bid: $87,500

**20177 George VI 10 Cents 1937,** KM34, MS67 PCGS. The 1937 10 Cents marks a change in the reverse design, in addition to the new monarch on the obverse. This "fishing schooner under sail" recently received official recognition as the famous Nova Scotia racing ship *Bluenose.* Variegated purple, tan, red, and light green toning envelops both sides. Scintillating satiny luster adds to the aesthetic appeal. Sharply struck and essentially pristine. This is the only MS67 graded by PCGS, with none finer (7/09).
*From the Canadiana Collection*
Estimate: $400-$600   Starting Bid: $200

**20178 George VI 10 Cents 1937,** KM34, Matte Specimen 67 PCGS. Struck for the first year of the reign of George VI from dies made at the Paris Mint. Interestingly, the 1937 has a date that is slightly smaller than subsequent George VI dimes. A total of 1,295 Specimens were minted. Although the exact distribution is unknown, both mirror and matte finishes were used for these special issues.

This piece has similar toning to the example in the Norweb Collection (Bowers and Merena, 11/1996, lot 251) that was originally from the King Farouk sale. Appealing light blue toning in the centers is surrounded by iridescent red-orange patina in the margins. Soft luster radiates from the immaculate surfaces. An attractive, nearly fully struck example. PCGS has certified just two pieces finer (7/09).
*From the Canadiana Collection*
Estimate: $450-$650   Starting Bid: $225

**20179 George VI 10 Cents 1938,** KM34, MS65 PCGS. Eye-catching violet, golden-brown, red, and teal toning dominates the southeast portion of the obverse and continues around the perimeter. The entire reverse is enveloped by magnificent rainbow toning, with blue, lavender, gold, and red throughout. Splendid satiny luster radiates from the colorful surfaces. Several wispy grazes on the King's cheek are consistent with the grade. This boldly struck Gem would make a fabulous addition to an advanced collection. PCGS Population: 10 in 65, 1 finer (7/09).
*From the Canadiana Collection*
Estimate: $600-$800   Starting Bid: $300

**20180 George VI 10 Cents 1939,** KM34, MS65 PCGS. Splashes of sea-green and lavender grace the margins of both sides. The reverse is particularly attractive, with prominent toning along the top. The resplendent surfaces show only a couple of insignificant abrasions. The strike is nearly full. An outstanding representative with above-average eye appeal. PCGS has graded only four examples finer (7/09).
*From the Canadiana Collection*
Estimate: $450-$650   Starting Bid: $225

**20181 George VI 10 Cents 1940,** KM34, MS65 ICCS. Dappled tan and violet toning covers both sides. A few minor marks are nearly imperceptible without a loupe. The strike is razor-sharp, and the eye appeal is excellent. This piece would make a splendid type coin, and it would be essentially impossible to locate a nicer example.
*From the Canadiana Collection*
Estimate: $200-$400   No Minimum Bid

**20182 George VI 10 Cents 1941,** KM34, MS67 PCGS. The 1941 is one of the most challenging George VI 10 Cents issues in high grades, and this stunning Superb Gem is the finest example PCGS has certified (7/09). Scintillating satiny luster radiates from the nearly pristine surfaces. Wafts of violet and beige enhance the mostly silver-gray surfaces. A sharply struck and appealing representative.
*From the Canadiana Collection*
Estimate: $1,250-$1,500   Starting Bid: $625

**20183 George VI 10 Cents 1942,** KM34, MS65 ICCS. This outstanding piece has been conservatively graded MS65 by ICCS. There are just a couple of insignificant marks, and the details are exquisitely defined. Pleasing violet toning around the margins yields to hints of red in the obverse center, while the reverse has more golden coloration. Shimmering satiny luster graces both sides. An outstanding representative.
*From the Canadiana Collection*
Estimate: $450-$650   Starting Bid: $225

**20184 George VI 10 Cents 1943,** KM34, MS65 PCGS. A colorfully toned Gem with lavender, yellow-gold, and light orange toning on both sides. The King's hair is a trifle soft, but other details are crisply defined. There are no significant marks. Radiant satiny luster shines from the fields. Housed in an early PCGS holder. PCGS has certified only two pieces finer (7/09).
*From the Canadiana Collection*
Estimate: $200-$400   No Minimum Bid

**20185 George VI 10 Cents 1944,** KM34, MS66 ICCS. Charming red-orange and violet patina drapes the periphery, while the central design elements are untoned. Eye-catching semi-prooflike reflectivity complements the boldly struck details. A number of striations are seen in the obverse fields, and there are only a couple of virtually microscopic marks. This attractive piece would make an excellent type coin.
*From the Canadiana Collection*
Estimate: $250-$450   No Minimum Bid

**20186 George VI 10 Cents 1945,** KM34, MS65 Cameo ICCS. The highly reflective fields show sharp contrast against the frosted devices. Both sides appear remarkably devoid of any contact, and the strike is needle-sharp. Splendid purple and red-orange colors intermingle on both sides of this eye-catching piece. The 1945 10 Cents is seldom seen in such a lofty level of preservation. This example will surely please even the most discerning eye.
*From the Canadiana Collection*
Estimate: $200-$400   No Minimum Bid

**20187 George VI 10 Cents 1946,** KM34, MS66 PCGS, Ex: Norweb. The Norweb catalog graded this piece MS67 and briefly described it as, "Mottled lilac and sunset colors. Gorgeous." To that we would add that the strike is nearly full, pleasing satiny luster appears throughout the attractively toned surfaces. An expertly preserved Premium Gem with excellent eye appeal. PCGS has certified only five examples in MS66, with none finer (7/09).
*From the Canadiana Collection*
Estimate: $400-$600   Starting Bid: $200

**20188 George VI 10 Cents 1947,** KM34, MS65 ICCS. A touch of light tan patina complements mostly silver-gray surfaces. Several wispy grazes do not affect the impressive satiny luster. A number of thin die cracks are seen on the reverse. The strike is complete throughout. The 1947 is not rare in the absolute sense, but Gems are seldom seen.
*From the Canadiana Collection*
Estimate: $350-$550   Starting Bid: $175

**20189 George VI 10 Cents 1947 Maple Leaf,** KM34, MS66 ICCS, Lacquered. A small maple leaf was added to the right of the date to distinguish this issue, as struck in 1948, from outdated dies. Although India had been granted independence in the middle of 1947, new dies without the ET IND: IMP: (and Emperor of India) had not arrived at the Royal Canadian Mint by the beginning of 1948. This piece is virtually brilliant, with just a faint hint of medium-brown on the rims and a touch of milky-tan on the sails. The surfaces are nearly prooflike, and there are only a couple of insignificant grazes. A sharply struck representative.
*From the Canadiana Collection*
Estimate: $150-$350   No Minimum Bid

**20190** **George VI 10 Cents 1948,** KM43, MS65 ICCS. Traces of beige toning enhance the nearly brilliant surfaces of this captivating Gem. Magnificent semi-prooflike reflectivity graces the fields and highlights the boldly struck design elements. The obverse is remarkably clean, and the reverse has only a few minuscule marks. The 1948 had a low mintage of just 422,741 pieces.
*From the Canadiana Collection*
Estimate: $400-$600  Starting Bid: $200

**20191** **George VI 10 Cents 1949,** KM43, MS66 PCGS. This absolutely stunning Premium Gem boasts spectacular prooflike fields that show slight contrast against partly frosted devices. Several minor handling marks preclude an even higher grade. A few patches of yellow and russet grace the mostly silver-gray surfaces. Powerfully struck with excellent eye appeal. PCGS Population: 3 in 66, 1 finer (7/09).
*From the Canadiana Collection*
Estimate: $200-$400  No Minimum Bid

**20192** **George VI 10 Cents 1950,** KM43, MS65 ICCS. This vibrantly toned Gem is a superior representative of the issue. Splendid violet toning around the margins blends nicely with deep red in the centers. Impressive luster shines beneath the attractive patina. There are no significant marks, and the details are nearly fully struck.
*From the Canadiana Collection*
Estimate: $200-$400  No Minimum Bid

**20193** **George VI 10 Cents 1951,** KM43, MS66 PCGS. Delicate hazel toning accents the virtually brilliant surfaces. A couple of tiny abrasions do not distract. Appealing glassy reflectivity enhances both sides. The strike is needle-sharp, save for a touch of weakness on the King's hair. PCGS has certified only three examples in MS66, with one finer (7/09).
*From the Canadiana Collection*
Estimate: $250-$450  No Minimum Bid

**20194** **George VI 10 Cents 1952,** KM43, MS66 PCGS. The 1952 was the final issue during the reign of George VI. Today, it is possibly the most available date in the George VI 10 Cents series, and this sharply struck piece would make a terrific type coin. Mottled violet, deep red-orange, and silver-gray toning embraces the highly lustrous surfaces. Several light abrasions are barely visible beneath the attractive toning, along with a few striations, as made, in the obverse margins. PCGS Population: 5 in 66, 0 finer (7/09).
*From the Canadiana Collection*
Estimate: $200-$400  No Minimum Bid

## 1858 Province of Canada 20 Cents MS66

**20195** **Victoria 20 Cents 1858,** KM4, MS66 PCGS. The largest of the Province of Canada denominations, the 20 Cents coin is also the only one not to survive to the post-Confederation era as a circulating coin; the 25 Cents denomination took its place. The Dominion of Canada made a point of removing the 20 Cents coins from circulation, and as a result, survivors are elusive today, though worn examples remain affordable. Mint State coins, however, present their own challenges. This Premium Gem, tied with one other for the finest certified by PCGS (7/09), has vibrant luster that swirls beneath orange, copper-tan, and sage patina. Slight striking softness on the portrait is redeemed by the overall eye appeal.
*From the Canadiana Collection*
Estimate: $15,000-$20,000  Starting Bid: $7,500

**20196  Victoria 25 Cents 1870 Obverse 2,** KM5, MS66 PCGS. This is the sole finest example certified at PCGS of this first-year issue. The reverse is pinkish-lilac with glints of ice-blue and amber predominating; the obverse "reverses" the palette, with copper, cinnamon, and amber-gold dominant against a pinkish center. Furthering the appeal, this is the Q2 obverse described in Charlton as "exceedingly rare," with a wave that breaks into three parts joining the brow just below the crown. A delightful and unimprovable example, boldly struck and with minimal contact.
*From the Canadiana Collection*
Estimate: $12,500-$15,000   Starting Bid: $6,250

**20197  Victoria 25 Cents 1871 Obverse 2,** KM5, MS65 PCGS. The lower left corner of the neckline is pointed—diagnostic for this obverse variety. The vast majority of the 400,000 quarters struck in 1871 saw extensive circulation, and Mint State examples are elusive. PCGS has certified only 17 Uncirculated examples, among which the present coin is the second finest (7/09).

Variegated purple, gunmetal-gray, gold, and blue toning embraces the surfaces. The reverse is particularly lustrous, but this obverse has plenty of reflectivity in the periphery. A few minor abrasions are nearly imperceptible beneath the deep patina. The strike is bold.
*From the Canadiana Collection*
Estimate: $7,500-$10,000   Starting Bid: $3,750

**20198  Victoria 25 Cents 1871-H Obverse 2,** KM5, MS64 PCGS. The portrait has the diagnostic pointed neckline. The 1871-H, like many issues in the Victoria 25 Cents series, is challenging even in low Mint State grades. Wafts of reddish-tan patina grace the surfaces of this lustrous near-Gem. The strike is bold, save for some softness on the high points of Victoria's hair. Several small marks are consistent with the grade. PCGS has certified only three finer examples (7/09).
*From the Canadiana Collection*
Estimate: $3,000-$4,000   Starting Bid: $1,500

**20199  Victoria 25 Cents 1872-H Obverse 2,** KM5, MS65 PCGS. The largest production of all the Victoria 25 Cents, hence a popular type coin, with a mintage recorded at 2.24 million pieces. Nonetheless more elusive in Gem grade than one might expect from the large production. This piece is one of only two so certified at PCGS, and there are none finer (7/09). This is a powder-gray piece, with pinkish accents around the device lettering joined by glints of ice-blue on the reverse. The surfaces show some orange-peel effect from moderate die erosion. A few small marks of little consequence apparently preclude a finer grade. Well struck and conditionally elusive.
*From the Canadiana Collection*
Estimate: $6,500-$8,500   Starting Bid: $3,250

**20200** **Victoria 25 Cents 1872-H Obverse 2,** KM5, Specimen 64 PCGS. A rare and highly desirable Specimen striking of this early 25 Cents. The obverse boasts an impressive prooflike sheen, while the reverse has a frosted center and moderate reflectivity in the margins. Splashes of purple, light blue, rose, and silver-gray cover most of the surfaces, with milky-white patina across the reverse center. Numerous die striations are particularly noticeable on the obverse, normal for the Specimen format. A fully struck and attractive example.

*From the Canadiana Collection*

Estimate: $5,000-$7,000   Starting Bid: $2,500

## Stunning MS67 1874-H Canada 25 Cents

20201 **Victoria 25 Cents 1874-H,** KM5, MS67 PCGS, Ex: Campbell. With a mintage of 1.6 million pieces, the 1874-H is among the more heavily produced Victoria 25 Cents, and in all grades it enjoys considerable popularity as a type coin. This Superb Gem certainly is an outstanding representative of the type, though perhaps a high-end date set is a more appropriate resting place for this charming coin. Lustrous peach-orange, silver-blue, and gray toning embraces each side of this pleasingly lustrous, of this slightly softly struck survivor. The sole finest example of the date known to PCGS (7/09). Sandy Campbell recognizes this piece as the best business strike Victorian quarter that he has seen or handled. *From the Canadiana Collection* Estimate: $75,000-$100,000 Starting Bid: $37,500

## Gorgeous MS64 1875-H 25 Cents

**20202  Victoria 25 Cents 1875-H,** KM5, MS64 PCGS, Blunt 5 in the date, Ex: Eliasberg. Through a combination of attrition and melting, the 1875-H 25 Cents was reduced to a relative handful of survivors, and collectors prize an example in any grade. The coins circulated to a great extent; the *PCGS Population Report* shows a cluster of certified survivors in VF grades. As that report also makes clear, Mint State examples are highly elusive. PCGS has graded only four Uncirculated pieces, with this MS64 survivor the best of the lot (7/09). The *Charlton Catalogue* for 2009 declines to price either variety for the date above AU50, apparently due to a lack of population data from the Canada-centered certification services.

The description given this piece at its last auction appearance, when Heritage offered selections from the world coins collected by Louis E. Eliasberg, Sr., still stands: "... fully original surfaces are blanketed with an ideal blend of soft gray and gold patina with full underlying mint brilliance. The reverse is virtually flawless while the obverse displays two tiny contact marks on the Queen's neck, mentioned for absolute accuracy. This fabulous coin will undoubtedly become one of the legendary pieces in the Canadian series." With this auction appearance, may the legend grow!
*From the Canadiana Collection*
Estimate: $75,000-$100,000  Starting Bid: $37,500

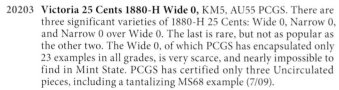

**20203  Victoria 25 Cents 1880-H Wide 0,** KM5, AU55 PCGS. There are three significant varieties of 1880-H 25 Cents: Wide 0, Narrow 0, and Narrow 0 over Wide 0. The last is rare, but not as popular as the other two. The Wide 0, of which PCGS has encapsulated only 23 examples in all grades, is very scarce, and nearly impossible to find in Mint State. PCGS has certified only three Uncirculated pieces, including a tantalizing MS68 example (7/09).

Light reddish-purple and hazel patina accents the margins, while the surfaces are otherwise pale gray. Victoria's hair shows typical minor weakness. Pleasing field luster is unaffected by scattered, grade-defining abrasions. A remarkable example of the highly desirable and seldom-seen variety.
*From the Canadiana Collection*
Estimate: $3,000-$5,000   Starting Bid: $1,500

**20204  Victoria 25 Cents 1880-H Narrow 0,** KM5, MS64 PCGS. The G's in the legend are defective at the bottom, as with the Wide 0 variety. This piece also has a missing lower left serif on the N and missing lower right serif on the A, both of REGINA. The I in GRATIA is boldly repunched. Although not as scarce as its Wide 0 counterpart, the 1880-H Narrow 0 is conditionally rare at this lofty level. PCGS has graded only three MS64 examples, with none finer (7/09).

Scintillating satiny luster drapes the lightly abraded surfaces. Delicate gold toning graces the margins. Victoria's hair is a trifle soft, but the details are crisp elsewhere. An appealing representative.
*From the Canadiana Collection*
Estimate: $7,500-$10,000   Starting Bid: $3,750

## Important Gem 1880-H 25 Cents Narrow 0 Over Wide 0

20205 **Victoria 25 Cents 1880-H Narrow 0 Over Wide 0,** KM5, MS65 PCGS. A distinct repunched date digit that is clear under magnification, wherein the Wide 0 was laid down first and then the Narrow 0 was applied over it. This is a highly important survivor. According to the *PCGS Population Report*, that service has graded just four examples of the variety: a Good 6, an XF40, an XF45—and this MS65 survivor, an astounding leap up from the next highest coin (7/09). The luster is lovely, filtering through rich silver-blue central toning that has green-gold and reddish-orange hints close to the rims. A coin whose importance should not be underestimated.

*From the Canadiana Collection*

Estimate: $17,500-$22,500  Starting Bid: $8,750

**20206 Victoria 25 Cents 1881-H Obverse 2,** KM5, MS64 PCGS. The Q2 Obverse apparently always appears on the 1881-H coinage. The first A in CANADA is boldly doubled. This Choice Mint State piece has satiny silver luster with pale gold toning at the borders. The surfaces are pleasing and free of significant marks. The 1881-H is considered a plentiful issue, although no Victoria 25 Cents pieces are common in the higher Mint State grades. This MS64 and a single MS67 are the only two coins that PCGS has certified above MS63. The Dominion Collection had a MS63, and the Belzberg Collection had an AU58.
*From the Canadiana Collection*
Estimate: $5,000-$7,000   Starting Bid: $2,500

**20207 Victoria 25 Cents 1882-H Obverse 3,** KM5, MS64 PCGS. Collectors who seek examples of each different portrait type must have this date, creating added demand. Both sides have mostly frosty silver luster. The obverse has light gold at the border, and the reverse has deeper gold and iridescent toning. PCGS has certified six examples in MS64 and one finer coin, a remarkable MS67 (7/09). This piece is two points finer than the Dominion and Belzberg coins, and far finer than the cleaned AU in the Norweb Collection.
*From the Canadiana Collection*
Estimate: $4,000-$6,000   Starting Bid: $2,000

**20208  Victoria 25 Cents 1883-H,** KM5, MS66 PCGS, Ex: Grossman. The single finest certified of this elusive issue, with a mintage of 960,000 coins. In fact there is only one piece each certified in MS65 and MS66 at PCGS, with nine in MS64 (7/09). The small amounts of silver minor coinage produced during the 1870s and 1880s circulated widely for the most part; the few Mint State survivors occurred by chance, were in collectors' sets, or were in the occasional hoard discovery. This piece offers pinkish-silver surfaces lightly accented with ice-blue, essentially pristine and well struck.
*From the Canadiana Collection*
Estimate: $12,000-$15,000   Starting Bid: $6,000

**20209  Victoria 25 Cents 1885 Obverse 2 Curved Top 5,** KM5, MS64 PCGS. The Q2 obverse is seen on all the business strikes. The 1885 25 Cents spent many years as an underrated issue, quietly circulating and steadily declining in availability, and by the time it was actively saved from circulation, only a handful of Mint State pieces existed. The *PCGS Population Report* shows just three coins tied for finest at MS64, including the present piece (7/09). Both sides have soft silver-gray luster dominant. Reddish-orange and steel-blue are visible at the obverse margins, while the reverse has a diagonal streak of green-gold that passes over the CE of CENTS and the first two date digits.
*From the Canadiana Collection*
Estimate: $17,500-$22,500   Starting Bid: $8,750

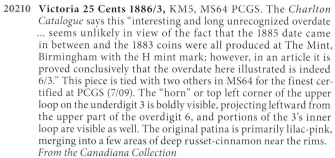

**20210**  **Victoria 25 Cents 1886/3,** KM5, MS64 PCGS. The *Charlton Catalogue* says this "interesting and long unrecognized overdate ... seems unlikely in view of the fact that the 1885 date came in between and the 1883 coins were all produced at The Mint, Birmingham with the H mint mark; however, in an article it is proved conclusively that the overdate here illustrated is indeed 6/3." This piece is tied with two others in MS64 for the finest certified at PCGS (7/09). The "horn" or top left corner of the upper loop on the underdigit 3 is boldly visible, projecting leftward from the upper part of the overdigit 6, and portions of the 3's inner loop are visible as well. The original patina is primarily lilac-pink, merging into a few areas of deep russet-cinnamon near the rims.
*From the Canadiana Collection*
Estimate: $7,500-$10,000   Starting Bid: $3,750

**20211**  **Victoria 25 Cents 1887,** KM5, AU58 PCGS. A rarity in the series. Only 100,000 of these coins were minted. The obverse of this brilliant silver piece is prooflike, and the reverse is frosty. There is only a trace of wear and no evidence of toning. PCGS has only certified one Mint State piece, an MS61. That coin is followed by this example and two other AU58 pieces (7/09). This 1887 is finer than the Norweb, Belzberg, and Dominion collection coins.
*From the Canadiana Collection*
Estimate: $6,500-$8,500   Starting Bid: $3,250

**20212  Victoria 25 Cents 1888 Narrow 8's,** KM5, MS64 PCGS. The Narrow 8 is a similar rarity to the Wide 8 variety. PCGS does not distinguish between the two and has certified only six pieces at the MS64 level, with none finer (7/09). Several letters and numerals show moderate repunching, including the N in CANADA, the 5 in the denomination, the CEN in CENTS, and the 1 in the date. Peppered purple toning and glints of lavender surround the gold and deep gray centers. Delightful luster accents the powerfully struck design elements. A carefully preserved and attractive representative.
*From the Canadiana Collection*
Estimate: $3,500-$5,000   Starting Bid: $1,750

**20213  Victoria 25 Cents 1889, Closed 9,** KM5, MS63 PCGS. Produced to the extent of only 66,340 coins, the 1889 is far and away the most elusive issue in the later Victoria 25 Cents series, as supported by the paltry PCGS population figures in Mint State—one MS62 and four MS63 coins, including the present piece, with none finer (7/09). The surfaces are a consistent pinkish-silver, deepening to a smattering of charcoal-gray in some of the lettering and devices at the rims. Only scattered, light contact marks are noted, making this piece quite high-end for the grade assigned. The Queen's neck and cheek are remarkably clean.
*From the Canadiana Collection*
Estimate: $9,000-$12,000   Starting Bid: $4,500

**20214  Victoria 25 Cents 1890H,** KM5, MS65 PCGS. The last Heaton production in the Victoria 25 Cents series, the only one with the Long Stem Ends design, produced to the extent of 200,000 coins. This is the sole MS65 certified at PCGS, although one MS66 is finer (7/09). A brilliant silver-gray piece with a full complement of luster on both sides, and just a hint of lilac patina near the rims. Sharp and delightful.
*From the Canadiana Collection*
Estimate: $7,500-$10,000   Starting Bid: $3,750

**20215  Victoria 25 Cents 1891,** KM5, MS66 PCGS. An impressively lustrous Premium Gem with silver-gray, tan-orange, and green-gold across each side. The devices are well-defined overall, and only a small flaw hidden in the lower left obverse field precludes an even finer designation. The eye appeal is simply fantastic. This later Victorian-era date has a mintage of just 120,000 pieces, and while a few Mint State examples are known, Gem and better coins are very rare. This MS66 representative is one of two tied for finest at PCGS (7/09).
*From the Canadiana Collection*
Estimate: $15,000-$20,000   Starting Bid: $7,500

**20216  Victoria 25 Cents 1892,** KM5, MS65 PCGS. Pleasing purple and gunmetal-gray patina covers the obverse, which contrasts nicely against the violet, blue, and reddish-gold toning that surrounds the silver-gray reverse center. Captivating satiny luster glimmers across both sides. A few insignificant luster grazes keep this piece from being absolutely flawless. The strike is razor-sharp. Tied for finest at PCGS with two other pieces (7/09).
*From the Canadiana Collection*
Estimate: $7,500-$10,000   Starting Bid: $3,750

## Remarkable MS66 1893 25 Cents—Single Finest at PCGS

**20217** **Victoria 25 Cents 1893,** KM5, MS66 PCGS. The 1893 is tied (with the 1887) for the second-lowest mintage among Victoria 25 Cents, and it commands a healthy sum in all grades. Despite its elusive nature, it does have minor availability in lesser Mint State grades, making it somewhat accessible. In Choice Mint State or finer, however, the 1893 25 Cents is flat-out rare. This Premium Gem stands alone atop the *PCGS Population Report* (7/09). Both sides are beautifully smooth, with frosty luster beneath silver-gray toning that shows glimpses of green, blue, peach, and heather. Strongly struck and memorably appealing.
*From the Canadiana Collection*
Estimate: $17,500-$22,500  Starting Bid: $8,750

20218  **Victoria 25 Cents 1894, Obverse 5b,** KM5, MS66 PCGS. Lightly toned silver-gray with blushes of pink and ivory at the rims. From the original mintage of a half-million coins, this example is tied for finest certified at PCGS with two other MS66 coins (7/09). The eye appeal is splendid, and the strike is excellent. The reverse is high-end even for the grade, despite a small dark fleck at the top of the E in CENTS. The Belzberg coin was an MS65 formerly in the Norweb Collection.
*From the Canadiana Collection*
Estimate: $8,500-$10,000   Starting Bid: $4,250

20219  **Victoria 25 Cents 1899,** KM5, MS65 PCGS. Lovely violet toning fills the fields, which contrast nicely against the lavender and silver-gray devices. Occasional wafts of teal and rose enhance the eye appeal. Coruscating satiny luster complements the well-struck design elements. Although easily located in most grades, the 1899 becomes scarce in Mint State. PCGS has certified only four examples in MS65, with one finer (7/09).
*From the Canadiana Collection*
Estimate: $3,500-$5,000   Starting Bid: $1,750

**20221**   **Victoria 25 Cents 1901,** KM5, MS64 PCGS. An appealing example of the final issue under Queen Victoria. Vibrant rose-gold and lavender toning covers both sides of this well-preserved piece. A few minuscule abrasions do not detract from the shimmering, satiny luster. Crisply struck with excellent eye appeal. Scarce any finer.
*From the Canadiana Collection*
Estimate: $1,200-$1,500   Starting Bid: $600

**20220**   **Victoria 25 Cents 1900,** KM5, MS67 PCGS. The 1900 is one of the most available Victoria 25 Cents, but as one might expect, it is seldom seen at this lofty level. This magnificent example is the finest certified by PCGS (7/09).

Scintillating satiny luster radiates beneath an attractive medley of light green, purple, steel-blue, red, and gold toning. Inspection with a loupe reveals only a couple of nearly imperceptible handling marks. The details are exquisitely defined.
*From the Canadiana Collection*
Estimate: $6,500-$8,500   Starting Bid: $3,250

20222 **Edward VII 25 Cents 1902, KM11, MS65 PCGS.** This is a popular first-year issue from the reign of Edward VII. From 1902 to 1910 the bust of Edward VII faced to the right, but that was changed when the obverse was redesigned in 1911. The obverse exhibits concentric circles of yellow, light green, blue, and hazel that cover the satiny fields, while the center is icy-frosted. A more even mix of blue, gold, and gray envelops the reverse. Several light marks on the King's forehead limit an even finer grade. PCGS Population: 2 in 65, 2 finer (7/09).
*From the Canadiana Collection*
Estimate: $5,500-$7,500  Starting Bid: $2,750

20223 **Edward VII 25 Cents 1902-H, KM11, MS66 PCGS.** The 1902-H is the only Heaton Mint issue in the entire Edward VII 25 Cents series. Dazzling satiny luster shines throughout the impeccably preserved surfaces. Splendid violet, sky-blue, reddish-gold, and gray toning drapes both sides. This boldly struck Premium Gem piece is a wonderful representative of the issue. PCGS has certified just one example finer (7/09).
*From the Canadiana Collection*
Estimate: $2,000-$3,000  Starting Bid: $1,000

20224 **Edward VII 25 Cents 1903,** KM11, MS65 PCGS. Despite a fairly substantial mintage of 846,150 pieces, the 1903 is elusive in Mint State. Gem examples are nearly impossible to find, and the connoisseur should not pass up this important opportunity. Shades of magenta, steel-blue, yellow-gold, lilac, and teal grace the surfaces. A few tiny marks are barely visible beneath the thick mint frost. Powerfully struck with excellent eye appeal. PCGS Population: 6 in 65, 4 finer (7/09).
*From the Canadiana Collection*
Estimate: $7,500-$10,000   Starting Bid: $3,750

## Gorgeous Premium Gem 1904 25 Cents

20225  **Edward VII 25 Cents 1904,** KM11, MS66 PCGS, Ex: Crouch-Cornwell. Outside of the Small Crown variant of the 1906 issue, the 1904 25 Cents is the most challenging Edwardian issue for the denomination. In the higher Mint State levels, however, the 1904 and surrounding dates are of nearly equal condition rarity. This excellent Premium Gem has pleasing overall detail. Strong luster shines through the rich violet and rose toning over each side, slightly thicker on the obverse. There are no individually mentionable flaws. PCGS Population: 4 in 66, 1 finer (7/09).
*From the Canadiana Collection*
Estimate: $20,000-$30,000  Starting Bid: $10,000

20226 **Edward VII 25 Cents 1905,** KM11, MS66 PCGS, Ex: Cornwell. Vibrant russet and hazel toning drapes most of both sides, with pleasing purple and silver-gray accents. Wonderful satiny luster highlights the razor-sharp design elements. The surfaces appear pristine to the unaided eye; inspection with a loupe reveals only a couple of pin-sized handling marks. PCGS has certified only three examples in MS66, with none finer (7/09).
*From the Canadiana Collection*
Estimate: $15,000-$20,000   Starting Bid: $7,500

20227 **Edward VII 25 Cents 1906 Large Crown,** KM11, MS65 PCGS. The Large Crown quarters constituted the vast majority of the 237,843 coins minted. Mottled violet, medium-brown, gold, and silver-gray toning envelops the lustrous surfaces. Several wispy abrasions blend well with the deep patina. It would be virtually impossible to locate an example nicer than this sharply struck Gem. PCGS Population: 4 in 65, 1 finer (7/09).
*From the Canadiana Collection*
Estimate: $7,500-$10,000   Starting Bid: $3,750

**20228 Edward VII 25 Cents 1906 Small Crown,** KM11, XF45 PCGS. The reverse was altered in 1906 to improve both the die life and the appearance of the coins. Apparently a very small number of pieces were struck using the old dies, and although the exact mintage is unknown, the Small Crown variety is many times rarer than its Large Crown counterpart. Charlton (2008) reports that "fewer than 35 examples of the 1906 Small Crown coin, across all grades, have been recorded." PCGS has certified only 10 examples in all grades, with just two pieces (AU55 and MS62) finer than the present coin (7/09).

Charming pale gray patina drapes both sides. A touch of verdigris is seen around a few of the obverse letters. Scattered abrasions define the grade, but none merit individual mention. An appealing example of this challenging issue. The serious collector should not miss this important opportunity.
*From the Canadiana Collection*
Estimate: $12,500-$15,000   Starting Bid: $6,250

**20229 Edward VII 25 Cents 1907,** KM11, MS66 PCGS. Dappled reddish-tan, steel-blue, and lavender toning envelops both sides of this highly lustrous Premium Gem. The strike is nearly full, and there are only a couple of inconsequential marks. Despite a plentiful mintage of more than 2 million coins, the 1907 25 Cents becomes rare in Gem and higher grades. PCGS Population: 2 in 66, 1 finer (7/09).
*From the Canadiana Collection*
Estimate: $6,500-$8,500   Starting Bid: $3,250

20230 **Edward VII 25 Cents 1908,** KM11, MS66 PCGS. After a robust mintage of more than 2 million pieces in 1907, the 1908 had a small emission of less than a half-million coins. Dazzling satiny luster radiates from the surfaces of this well-preserved example. A ring of gold and pale blue surrounds the brilliant obverse center, while the reverse has splashes of hazel patina. This crisply struck Premium Gem has no significant marks. PCGS has certified only four examples at the MS66 level, with none finer (7/09).
*From the Canadiana Collection*
Estimate: $4,000-$6,000   Starting Bid: $2,000

20231 **Edward VII 25 Cents 1909,** KM11, MS65 PCGS. The 1909 is one of the most difficult Edward VII 25 Cents to locate in high grades. In fact, with the exception of the rare 1906 Small Crown issue, this is the only date for which Charlton (2008) attempts no value estimate. What this magnificent piece sells for is really anyone's guess. It will undoubtedly be treasured by whoever is lucky enough to own it.

A lovely mix of yellow-gold, pumpkin-orange, red, and lilac patina graces the left side of the obverse, while the right side has a bright silver-gray area. The reverse exhibits a similar toning pattern. Several nearly imperceptible marks keep this piece from being absolutely flawless. A highly lustrous and attractive representative. PCGS Population: 2 in 65, 0 finer (7/09).
*From the Canadiana Collection*
Estimate: $9,000-$12,000   Starting Bid: $4,500

**20233  George V 25 Cents 1911**, KM18, MS66 PCGS. Although ridiculed at the time, the 1911 coins, with their "Godless" obverse, are highly popular among collectors today. The present coin is an outstanding example of this one-year type with vibrant rainbow toning. An arc of deep blue and violet drapes the southeast regions of both sides and halfway up the rims. The bottom obverse also has lime-green, rose-gold, and magenta accents. Layered golden-brown, yellow, rose-red, and steel-blue toning dominates the centers of both sides. Fantastic satiny luster shines throughout the carefully preserved surfaces. This boldly struck piece exudes eye appeal. PCGS Population: 9 in 66, 2 finer (7/09).
*From the Canadiana Collection*
Estimate: $1,250-$1,500   Starting Bid: $625

**20232  Edward VII 25 Cents 1910**, KM11a, MS66 PCGS. The weight of the 25 Cents was slightly increased in 1910 from 5.81 to 5.83 gm. This year was also the final issue under the reign of Edward VII. Lovely cobalt-blue, purple, deep red, and gold toning drapes both sides of this sharply struck Premium Gem. The highly lustrous surfaces appear nearly pristine to the unaided eye. PCGS Population: 3 in 66, 0 finer (7/09).
*From the Canadiana Collection*
Estimate: $3,500-$5,000   Starting Bid: $1,750

**20234  George V 25 Cents 1912,** KM24, MS65 PCGS. Pleasing blue-green and reddish-gold toning accents both sides, mostly at the margins. Several light grazes barely affect the impressive satiny luster. The crown is a trifle soft, but the other details are boldly struck. The 1912 is seldom seen in Gem condition. PCGS Population 3 in 65, 1 finer (7/09).
*From the Canadiana Collection*
Estimate: $2,500-$3,500   Starting Bid: $1,250

**20235  George V 25 Cents 1913,** KM24, MS66 PCGS. The 1913 is surprisingly scarce in high grades despite a plentiful mintage of more than 2 million pieces. PCGS has graded only two examples in MS66, with none finer (7/09). Deep purple toning surrounds the lightly frosted and untoned centers of this well-preserved Premium Gem. There are just a few insignificant luster grazes, and the strike is nearly full.
*From the Canadiana Collection*
Estimate: $3,000-$5,000   Starting Bid: $1,500

**20236  George V 25 Cents 1914,** KM24, MS66 PCGS. As a glance at the population data indicates, the 1914 25 Cents becomes scarce in Uncirculated grades. Examples are extremely difficult to find above Choice Mint State. In fact, Charlton (2008) lists no price above MS64. PCGS has certified only one piece in MS65. and the present piece is the only MS66, with none finer (7/09). As the single finest certified example of a conditionally rare issue, this piece should be subject to fierce bidder competition.

Lovely cobalt-blue and lavender toning surrounds the rose-gold obverse center. The reverse is nearly covered by deep blue, green, and purple patina. Shimmering satiny luster highlights the powerfully impressed design elements. A few pin-sized obverse abrasions are visible under magnification, but the reverse is virtually mark-free. This magnificent piece will suit even the most discerning eye.
*From the Canadiana Collection*
Estimate: $7,000-$10,000   Starting Bid: $3,500

**20237  George V 25 Cents 1915,** KM24, MS65 PCGS, Ex: Ferguson-Norweb. The sole finest example of the date certified by PCGS (7/09) and a longstanding claimant to that title, as the green label holder evinces. Both sides of this lustrous beauty are largely silver-white with a hint of blue; only a smattering of sage at the lower left obverse margin is a distinctly different color. As a rule, the 25 Cents coins struck during George V's reign circulated heavily. The low-mintage 1915 issue received no particular attention until decades after its striking, by which time only a handful of unworn coins existed. In the Norweb sale, the cataloger described this coin as a "legend-to-be," and in the context of this magnificent collection, the legend has become truth.
*From the Canadiana Collection*
Estimate: $15,000-$20,000   Starting Bid: $7,500

20238 **George V 25 Cents 1916,** KM24, MS66 PCGS. Yellow-gold accents the mostly pale gray centers, while the margins boast violet, blue, and red toning. Delightful satiny luster enhances the nearly perfect surfaces. This attractive and nearly fully struck Premium Gem is an issue that is rare above MS64. Even low-Mint State examples are seldom offered. PCGS Population: 2 in 66, 0 finer (7/09).
*From the Canadiana Collection*
Estimate: $2,000-$3,000 Starting Bid: $1,000

20239 **George V 25 Cents 1917,** KM24, MS67 PCGS. The 1917 25 Cents is difficult to find above MS64. This terrific Superb Gem is the sole finest example PCGS has certified (7/09). Eye-catching yellow-gold, rose-red, green, and lavender blend nicely across the surfaces, completely covering the reverse, while the obverse has some silver-gray remaining. Magnificent satiny luster complements the razor-sharp design elements. Both sides are virtually perfect, and only a couple of minuscule handling marks appear under a glass.
*From the Canadiana Collection*
Estimate: $4,000-$6,000 Starting Bid: $2,000

20240  **George V 25 Cents 1918,** KM24, MS67 PCGS. A carefully preserved piece with appealing multicolored toning— violet and
cobalt-blue in the centers, with rose-red, teal, and iridescent yellow-gold at the rims. The strike is full, and magnification reveals
only a few minor marks. Flashy luster shines beneath the attractive
toning. This is the single finest example PCGS has graded (7/09).
*From the Canadiana Collection*
Estimate: $4,000-$6,000   Starting Bid: $2,000

20241  **George V 25 Cents 1919,** KM24, MS66 PCGS. The final issue
struck with a sterling (.925) fineness. A delightful lilac hue
embraces the obverse, which contrasts nicely against the gold-
tinted, purple-speckled reverse. Splendid satiny luster shimmers
throughout. Several insignificant marks preclude an even higher
grade. PCGS has certified only five MS66 examples, with none
finer (7/09).
*From the Canadiana Collection*
Estimate: $900-$1,200   Starting Bid: $450

20242  **George V 25 Cents 1920,** KM24a, MS67 PCGS. This outstanding coin is the sole finest PCGS has certified (7/09). None have
been graded MS66, and there are only nine pieces in MS65. With
a grade two points higher than the next-finest coins, this superior example represents a significant opportunity for collectors.

Pleasing cobalt-blue, purple, red, and gold patina drapes both
sides of this well-preserved Superb Gem. Captivating satiny luster
highlights the powerfully struck design elements. A couple of
pin-sized handling marks blend well with the deep toning, and
the strike is nearly full. This fabulous piece belongs in an important cabinet of Canadian coins.
*From the Canadiana Collection*
Estimate: $6,000-$8,000   Starting Bid: $3,000

**20243** **George V 25 Cents 1921,** KM24a, MS66 PCGS, Ex: Prince-Nemethy. With a mintage of just under 600,000 pieces, the 1921 25 Cents has a respectably low mintage, though other years saw fewer George V coins struck. What sets the 1921 25 Cents apart is its degree of condition rarity, particularly in Mint State, where it trails only the elusive 1915 as most valuable in its class. This MS66 survivor, one of just three tied for finest certified by PCGS (7/09), is profoundly lustrous beneath pleasing patina, green-gold and sage at the peripheries, with silver-gray over the centers. An exquisite survivor and a remarkable opportunity for the condition-conscious collector.
*From the Canadiana Collection*
Estimate: $10,000-$12,000   Starting Bid: $5,000

**20244** **George V 25 Cents 1927,** KM24a, MS67 PCGS, Ex: Norweb. A standout survivor that is two grade points higher than its nearest rival in the *PCGS Population Report* (7/09). Superb Gems are at the pinnacle of preservation for the George V 25 Cents coins, with no more than one or two known to PCGS for each date and only 15 total graded by that firm. That a coin of this quality came from a mintage of less than a half-million pieces makes its existence even more remarkable. Rich peach, orange, and silver-gray spread across the centers, with heather and plum at the margins. A bold strike and vibrant luster complete the eye appeal.
*From the Canadiana Collection*
Estimate: $10,000-$12,000   Starting Bid: $5,000

**20245  George V 25 Cents 1928,** KM24a, MS67 PCGS. Speckled gold, blue, violet, and red toning accents the perimeter, while the central devices are silver-gray. Shimmering satiny luster complements the powerfully impressed design elements. The surfaces are virtually flawless. The 1928 25 Cents is elusive above Choice Mint State, and this appealing piece is the single finest example PCGS has certified (7/09).
*From the Canadiana Collection*
Estimate: $4,000-$6,000   Starting Bid: $2,000

**20246  George V 25 Cents 1929,** KM24a, MS66 PCGS. Dappled hazel, lilac, maroon, and silver-gray toning covers both sides, with deeper patination around the perimeter. Remarkable satiny luster complements the boldly struck design elements. A few tiny abrasions are nearly imperceptible to the unaided eye. The 1929 is virtually impossible to locate in a higher grade. PCGS Population: 5 in 66, 1 finer (7/09).
*From the Canadiana Collection*
Estimate: $2,000-$3,000   Starting Bid: $1,000

20247  **George V 25 Cents 1930,** KM24a, MS66 PCGS. As its mintage of less than 1 million coins would suggest, the 1930 is a relatively scarce issue, particularly in high grades. At the MS66 level, PCGS has certified only five pieces, with none finer (7/09). Hints of apricot-gold patina grace the periphery, while the centers are light silver-gray. The strike is nearly full, and there are no significant marks. An appealing representative.
*From the Canadiana Collection*
Estimate: $2,500-$3,500   Starting Bid: $1,250

20248  **George V 25 Cents 1931,** KM24a, MS66 PCGS. Violet and red patina covers the rims, contrasting nicely against silver-gray centers. Scintillating satiny luster highlights the exquisitely defined design elements. Both sides have only a few inconsequential grazes. PCGS Population: 1 in 66, 1 finer (7/09).
*From the Canadiana Collection*
Estimate: $3,000-$5,000   Starting Bid: $1,500

**20250 George V 25 Cents 1933,** KM24a, MS66 PCGS. A hint of lilac and gold toning around the margins mixes with the mostly silver-gray surfaces. Several wispy grazes keep this sharply struck piece from Superb Gem. This lustrous example would make a lovely addition to any collection. PCGS Population: 9 in 66, 1 finer (7/09).
*From the Canadiana Collection*
Estimate: $1,500-$2,000   Starting Bid: $750

**20249 George V 25 Cents 1932,** KM24a, MS67 PCGS. The 1932 25 Cents had a mintage of barely 500,000 pieces, and examples are rare above Choice Mint State. PCGS has graded only three pieces in MS65, and one each in MS66 and MS67, making this Superb Gem the single finest certified (7/09). Delightful orange-gold, lavender, russet, rose-gold, and silver-gray toning embraces both sides. The resplendent surfaces have only a couple of tiny marks that keep this piece from being absolutely flawless. The strike is needle-sharp. The perfect coin for the specialist.
*From the Canadiana Collection*
Estimate: $4,500-$5,500   Starting Bid: $2,250

**20251 George V 25 Cents 1934,** KM24a, MS67 PCGS. Coruscating satiny luster shines beneath the delightful patina. Gold, lilac, and silver-gray grace the obverse, with a lavender, reddish-gold, light green, and steel-blue reverse. This resplendent Superb Gem has razor-sharp devices and no significant marks. PCGS has certified only two examples in MS67, with none finer (7/09).
*From the Canadiana Collection*
Estimate: $4,000-$6,000   Starting Bid: $2,000

**20252 George V 25 Cents 1935,** KM24a, MS66 PCGS. At first glance this piece appears fully brilliant, but a closer inspection reveals a trace of tan toning. Wonderful satiny luster shines from the well-preserved surfaces. A loupe locates just a couple of tiny marks. Numerous die polish lines are seen at the reverse periphery. A boldly struck piece with great eye appeal. PCGS Population: 5 in 66, 0 finer (7/09).
*From the Canadiana Collection*
Estimate: $1,200-$1,500   Starting Bid: $600

**20253 George V 25 Cents 1936,** KM24a, MS67 PCGS. While the 1936 25 Cents can be located in most grades with a little patience, it may be years—even decades—before the collector can locate an example as nice as the present coin. In fact, this stunning Superb Gem is the single finest piece PCGS has certified (7/09). Mottled violet toning in the recesses blends nicely with reddish-gold patina that fills the fields and covers the devices. Dazzling satiny luster complements the powerfully impressed design elements. Inspection with a loupe reveals only a couple of pin-sized handling marks. The serious collector should not miss this important opportunity.
*From the Canadiana Collection*
Estimate: $4,000-$6,000   Starting Bid: $2,000

**20254 George V 25 Cents 1936 Bar,** KM24a, MS66 PCGS. The so-called "Bar" on this variety is actually a small die-break on the reverse that connects the ribbons. The 1936 25 Cents was the last issue of the denomination minted during George V's reign, although the elusive Dot coinage was struck from the same dies. A variegated mix of violet, red, green, gold, and hazel covers both sides. Magnificent satiny luster shimmers beneath the attractive toning. The strike is razor-sharp, and there are only a couple of grade-defining abrasions. An outstanding piece. PCGS has certified only one example finer (7/09).
*From the Canadiana Collection*
Estimate: $6,000-$7,500   Starting Bid: $3,000

**20255 George V 25 Cents 1936 Dot,** KM24a, MS65 PCGS. By the beginning of 1937 the Royal Canadian Mint had not received the new dies of George VI, but urgent demands for quarters necessitated an emergency issue using the old dies. To distinguish these coins, which were struck about a year after George V had died, a small raised dot was placed on the reverse below the wreath. Although there are also a handful of 1936 Dot Cents and dimes known, they all appear to have been Specimen strikes. The 1936 Dot 25 Cents, however, was struck in both Specimen and business strike formats.

Patches of lilac accent the mostly silver-gray surfaces. Flashy luster highlights the razor-sharp design elements. Several minuscule abrasions are consistent with the grade. The 1936 Dot 25 Cents is significantly scarcer than its non-Dot counterpart, with an estimated mintage (Krause) of 153,322 coins. Gem examples are rare, and it would be virtually impossible to find a better representative than the present coin. PCGS has certified only three examples at the MS65 level, with one finer (7/09).
*From the Canadiana Collection*
Estimate: $7,500-$10,000   Starting Bid: $3,750

# Remarkable George V 1936 Dot 25 Cents Specimen 68

**20256** **George V 25 Cents 1936 Dot,** KM24a, Specimen 68 PCGS. The abdication of Edward VIII at the end of 1936 precipitated not only a crisis in the British monarchy, it was also responsible for a coin shortage in Canada that resulted in the creation of some of the most revered treasures in the whole of Canadian numismatics—the 1936 Dot 1 Cent, 10 Cents, and 25 Cents. As was common practice in British coinage, when George V died in January 1936 the portrait of the deceased king continued in use during that year while the British Royal Mint began working on coinage dies for 1937 featuring the portrait of his son and successor, Edward VIII. Unpredictably (and astonishingly at the time), Edward VIII abandoned the throne in December 1936 in order to marry the twice-divorced American socialite Wallis Simpson. Edward VIII was succeeded by his brother Albert, who assumed the throne as George VI. Edward VIII remains the only British monarch who has ever voluntarily renounced the throne.

Upon Edward's abdication, the trial coinage dies bearing his portrait were invalid. (Side note: Edward VIII even contravened the numismatic tradition that an incoming British sovereign always faced the opposite direction on coinage from the previous monarch, insisting that his left profile was his best.) A severe shortage in Canada that arose in early 1937 of 1 Cent, 10 Cent, and 25 Cent coins produced the need to continue those denominations bearing the old George V portrait. To mark the 1936-dated coins as 1937 productions, a small dot was placed on the dies.

While the 1 Cent and 10 Cent coins are known only as Specimen strikings, the 1936 Dot 25 Cents are somewhat available (and extremely popular) in circulation strike format—a situation that, in itself, probably makes this incredible Specimen-68 coin even more desirable, as it is an issue that has tended to be underrated in the past when compared to the other Dot coinage.

This piece is untoned throughout and has splendid, somewhat satiny luster over the silver-white surfaces. It is an unquestioned Specimen striking, with high, squared-off rims and a *forceful* impression throughout, completely unlike the business strike 25 Cents, the vast majority of which show notable softness at the CA in CANADA. This coin can be identified for pedigree purposes by a quite shallow planchet lamination, visible in the reverse field between a leaf tip and the 1 in the date.

While we have been unable to track down detailed provenances, we believe this example may represent a recent discovery of a fifth Specimen 25 Cents. It was long believed that only three or four Specimens each existed of the 1 Cent, 10 Cents, and 25 Cents, and yet a new, fifth Specimen of the 10 Cents was discovered in 2000 when it was sold by a mint employee (who was at that time more than 90 years old) to a private collector. In Specimen 68 this coin is one of only two so certified at PCGS, and there are no Specimen 25 Cents in any other grade at that service (7/09). This coin is a remarkable find and an incredibly appealing chance to acquire one of the bedrock rarities of Canadian numismatics.
*From the Canadiana Collection*
Estimate: $90,000-$120,000 Starting Bid: $45,000

**20257** **George VI 25 Cents 1937,** KM35, MS66 PCGS. The new 1937 George VI quarters featured a caribou head on the reverse in an attempt to give the coins a more modern design. Vibrant violet, sky-blue, rose, and gold intermingle on the surfaces of this carefully preserved Premium Gem. Several wispy, insignificant abrasions are consistent with the grade. This razor-sharp piece has terrific eye appeal. PCGS has certified only two MS66 examples, with none finer (7/09).
*From the Canadiana Collection*
Estimate: $250-$550 No Minimum Bid

**20260** **George VI 25 Cents 1939,** KM35, MS66 PCGS. A delightful array of cobalt-blue, teal, and violet patina embraces the perimeter, while the fields have pleasing red-orange accents. Subtle rose toning graces the central design elements. Scintillating satiny luster adds to the aesthetic appeal of this fabulous representative. Several wispy grazes are nearly imperceptible without magnification. PCGS has certified only two examples in MS66, with none finer (7/09).
*From the Canadiana Collection*
Estimate: $700-$1,000 Starting Bid: $350

**20258** **George VI 25 Cents 1937,** KM35, Matte Specimen 67 PCGS, Ex: Pittman. The cataloger of the Pittman sale wrote: "Specimen sets of 1937 [were] issued to commemorate the coronation of the new King. Most of the 1,295 sets issued were the matte variety with probably only about 10 percent the mirrored variety ... ." Subtle gold patina in the margins blends with the mostly silver-gray surfaces. The fields show numerous die polish lines but are devoid of any marks. The strike is full. An excellent piece for the serious collector. PCGS Population: 8 in 67, 2 finer (7/09).
*From the Canadiana Collection*
Estimate: $300-$500 Starting Bid: $150

**20261** **George VI 25 Cents 1940,** KM35, MS66 PCGS. Deep purple and russet mingle with silver-gray on the obverse, while the reverse displays steel-blue and rose-gold. This exquisitely struck Premium Gem has only a couple of minor abrasions. Impressive luster radiates from the fields. An appealing representative. PCGS Population: 3 in 66, 0 finer (7/09).
*From the Canadiana Collection*
Estimate: $350-$550 Starting Bid: $175

**20259** **George VI 25 Cents 1938,** KM35, MS66 PCGS. Iridescent purple and electric blue patina surrounds mottled magenta toning at the obverse center. The reverse displays varied blue and purple shades. This gorgeous piece boasts eye-catching satiny luster. A few tiny marks blend with the attractive patina. This spectacular coin is the finest PCGS has certified (7/09) and is a coin its future owner will treasure.
*From the Canadiana Collection*
Estimate: $1,000-$1,300 Starting Bid: $500

**20262** **George VI 25 Cents 1941,** KM35, MS66 PCGS. Green, violet, lilac, blue, red, and hazel blend over the surfaces of this virtually immaculate Premium Gem. Coruscating satiny luster shines from both sides. This boldly struck piece has excellent eye appeal. PCGS has certified only five MS66 examples, and none are finer (7/09).
*From the Canadiana Collection*
Estimate: $350-$550 Starting Bid: $175

**20263** **George VI 25 Cents 1942,** KM35, MS66 PCGS. A trace of tan patina adds color to this mostly brilliant Premium Gem. Spectacular satiny luster enhances the eye appeal. The strike is razor-sharp, and there are only a couple of insignificant handling marks. The 1942 is seldom seen in such a lofty level of preservation. PCGS reports just two examples in MS66, with none finer (7/09).
*From the Canadiana Collection*
Estimate: $400-$600   Starting Bid: $200

**20264** **George VI 25 Cents 1943,** KM35, MS66 PCGS. The 1943 had the highest mintage of any George VI 25 Cents and is easily found in most grades. The present coin, however, is one of only a half-dozen in this highest grade at PCGS, and it exhibits eye appeal that is far above average. Captivating purple, red, and yellow-gold envelops the satiny surfaces. Several wispy grazes are undistracting. This attractive piece would make an excellent addition to an important collection. PCGS has certified no finer examples (7/09).
*From the Canadiana Collection*
Estimate: $400-$600   Starting Bid: $200

**20265** **George VI 25 Cents 1944,** KM35, MS66 PCGS. Shimmering satiny luster radiates beneath the steel-blue, lavender, and orange-gold patina that covers both sides. A couple of minuscule abrasions are consistent with the grade, and none are bothersome. This powerfully struck representative boasts tremendous eye appeal. PCGS has certified only two pieces at the MS66 level, and none finer (7/09).
*From the Canadiana Collection*
Estimate: $450-$650   Starting Bid: $225

**20266** **George VI 25 Cents 1945,** KM35, MS66 PCGS. This brilliant Premium Gem has deeply mirrored fields that show stunning cameo contrast against the frosted devices. The fields are decidedly prooflike, and at first glance this coin appears to be a Specimen strike. The details are boldly struck, and there are only a few tiny marks on each side. This is the single finest piece PCGS has encapsulated (7/09), a remarkable example that would be a highlight of any collection.
*From the Canadiana Collection*
Estimate: $450-$650   Starting Bid: $225

**20267** **George VI 25 Cents 1946,** KM35, MS66 PCGS. Pleasing apricot-gold and deep red toning mixes with silver-gray on both sides of this resplendent Premium Gem. The highly lustrous surfaces appear pristine to the unaided eye. The strike is needle-sharp. Although the 1946 25 Cents can be found in MS65 with little difficulty, MS66 examples are rare. PCGS has certified only five examples in that lofty level, and none finer (7/09).
*From the Canadiana Collection*
Estimate: $500-$700   Starting Bid: $250

**20268** **George VI 25 Cents 1947,** KM35, MS65 PCGS. A touch of gold and red surrounds the brilliant obverse center. The reverse is more colorful, with additional cobalt-blue and violet accents near the rims. Both sides exhibit captivating, watery reflectivity. The strike is bold, and there are only a few insignificant grazes. The 1947 25 Cents is surprisingly scarce in high grades; Gems are seldom seen. This piece is one of three such at PCGS, with none finer (7/09).
*From the Canadiana Collection*
Estimate: $1,500-$2,000   Starting Bid: $750

**20269** **George VI 25 Cents 1947 Dot,** KM35, MS65 PCGS. After India was granted its independence in 1947, the ET IND: IMP: (and Emperor of India) became outdated. New dies had to be made—a time-consuming process—and in the meantime the Royal Canadian Mint had to make do with old dies. To distinguish those issues a tiny maple leaf was placed to the right of the date. On an unknown number of examples, the maple leaf became filled and had the appearance of a tiny dot. Although this issue is more of a die state than a distinct variety, it is highly popular among collectors. Examples are scarce in all grades, and Gems are rarely offered.

Deep purplish-blue and red toning envelops the fields and margins, while the design elements are mostly silver-gray. Flashy luster shines beneath the lovely patina. The strike is razor-sharp, and there are only a few grade-defining abrasions. PCGS has certified just four pieces in MS65, with none finer (7/09).
*From the Canadiana Collection*
Estimate: $3,500-$5,000  Starting Bid: $1,750

**20270** **George VI 25 Cents 1947 Maple Leaf,** KM35, MS65 PCGS. Remarkable satiny luster shines from this virtually brilliant piece. There is just a hint of tan patina near the obverse rim. This resplendent Gem boasts powerfully struck details and clean surfaces. A loupe locates only a few nearly microscopic abrasions. An excellent example of this historically significant issue.
*From the Canadiana Collection*
Estimate: $250-$450  No Minimum Bid

**20271** **George VI 25 Cents 1947 Maple Leaf,** KM35, MS66 PCGS. The 1947 Maple Leaf was the final issue struck before a new obverse hub, with an updated legend, was prepared. The present coin has just a touch of milky-white patina on the mostly silver-gray surfaces. Shimmering satiny luster complements the razor-sharp design elements. A couple of light grazes keep this piece from an even higher grade. PCGS has certified nine MS66 examples, with none finer (7/09).
*From the Canadiana Collection*
Estimate: $350-$550  Starting Bid: $175

**20272** **George VI 25 Cents 1948,** KM44, MS67 PCGS—this piece appears to be a Specimen strike. The deeply mirrored fields and icy-frosted devices combine to create vivid cameo contrast. Delicate rose and pale blue toning adds color to this nearly brilliant representative. The surfaces appear immaculate to the unaided eye. This exquisitely detailed piece is sure to please the connoisseur.
*From the Canadiana Collection*
Estimate: $500-$750  Starting Bid: $250

**20273  George VI 25 Cents 1949,** KM44, MS67 PCGS—this piece appears to be a Specimen strike. A touch of dusty-gray patina and a few dots of russet accent the mostly brilliant surfaces. The surfaces boast intense prooflike reflectivity, with deeply mirrored fields. This sharply struck Superb Gem has only a couple of light handling marks.
*From the Canadiana Collection*
Estimate: $400-$600   Starting Bid: $200

**20274  George VI 25 Cents 1950,** KM44, MS65 PCGS. A pleasing golden hue graces the surfaces of this boldly struck Gem. Vivid semi-prooflike reflectivity enhances the appeal. A thin mark on George's forehead is barely worthy of mention. It would be virtually impossible to locate a better example of this date. PCGS Population: 5 in 65, 1 finer (7/09).
*From the Canadiana Collection*
Estimate: $300-$500   Starting Bid: $150

**20275  George VI 25 Cents 1951 High Relief,** KM44, MS65 PCGS. Concerning the 1951 and 1952 varieties, the *Charlton Catalogue* (2008) states:

"In an attempt to improve the appearance of the obverse of this denomination a fresh reduction was made to produce an obverse with a slightly larger, lower relief portrait. Both varieties were used in 1951 and 1952. Aside from the difference in relief and the size of the portrait, the two varieties can be distinguished by the lettering."

 The so-called High Relief issues are otherwise virtually identical to the previous George VI quarters. Variegated lilac, deep red, gold, magenta, and silver-gray toning envelops both sides. Dazzling semi-prooflike luster complements the sharply impressed design elements. Several minor abrasions are barely noticeable. PCGS has certified only six MS65 High Relief examples, with none finer (7/09).
*From the Canadiana Collection*
Estimate: $350-$550   Starting Bid: $175

**20276  George VI 25 Cents 1952 High Relief,** KM44, MS65 PCGS. Despite a relatively large mintage, the 1952 High Relief is surprisingly scarce in Mint State grades. The present coin is the single finest example PCGS has certified (7/09). This resplendent Gem boasts magnificent satiny luster. A trace of rose-red near the rims enhances the mostly brilliant obverse, while the reverse has pleasing sky-blue and lavender accents. Light, grade-consistent abrasions do not diminish the tremendous eye appeal.
*From the Canadiana Collection*
Estimate: $350-$550   Starting Bid: $175

## Monumental Victoria 1870 No LCW 50 Cents

**20277  Victoria 50 Cents 1870 No LCW,** KM6, MS64 PCGS, Ex: Miller-Alston-Grossman. A monumental example of this, one of the most coveted issues in all of Canadian numismatics. Although a business strike, this piece is tied numerically finest with the Belzberg coin, a unique piece certified Specimen 64 by both PCGS and ICCS. We wrote in the Belzberg catalog (Heritage, 1/2003, lot 15470), "Extremely rare in all grades, and a classic rarity in the Canadian 50 Cent series. Neither the Pittman nor Norweb collections had a Mint State example of this rare type, and PCGS has certified only two examples in Mint State."

Six years later that statement is still true: PCGS has certified only the present MS64 and one MS60 coin in Mint State, a piece that we handled in our September 2006 Long Beach World Coin Signature (lot 50457, which brought $25,300 against an estimate of $15,000-$17,500). The Belzberg Specimen brought a strong $103,500 in January 2003 against a top estimate of $100,000.

This incredible near-Gem coin is equally remarkable for its lovely original patina, with pastel lilac accented by dots of azure on the obverse. The reverse has more intense color, with a similar palette to the obverse around the periphery but vivid amber-gold predominating inside the wreath. The strike is quite sharp overall, although minor softness shows on the high points of the obverse hair. Neither that nor the few scattered contact marks detract from what must be far and away the most attractive and desirable business strike known—or imaginable—for this rare issue.

The 1870 Victoria 50 Cents were the first half dollars struck for Canada, only three years after the Confederation Act united four provinces into the Dominion of Canada. The various series issues were struck at the Royal Mint in London or the Heaton Mint in Birmingham, the latter bearing the familiar H mintmark. As the Province of Canada issued no half dollars, new dies were needed when the denomination was introduced. The dies were, unsurprisingly, designed by Leonard Charles Wyon, who was born in 1826 in one of the houses of the Royal Mint. The first-year 1870 half dollars were produced in two different obverse variants, with and without the designer's initials LCW on the truncation of the Queen's neck. The No LCW coins also lack a small shamrock behind the first jewel at the front of the crown, and other minor differences appear on that side as well.

This coin is now among the highlights of this wonderful collection, but it will continue to be a future cornerstone of even the most advanced Canadian collection for some forthright bidder. An opportunity that will almost certainly not be seen again soon.
*From the Canadiana Collection*
Estimate: $150,000-$200,000  Starting Bid: $75,000

## Landmark Gem Victoria 1870 LCW 50 Cents

20278 **Victoria 50 Cents 1870 LCW,** KM6, MS65 PCGS, Ex: Alston-Grossman. The second variety of this elusive first-year issue, here with the initials of designer Leonard C. Wyon on the neck truncation of Queen Victoria. This phenomenal Gem is tied for finest with only two other pieces in MS65 at PCGS (7/09). While the 1870 With LCW 50 Cents are considerably more available than the No LCW coins, both are extremely rare in Mint State, especially the Gem level of the present example.

With lovely original lilac to violet patina covering both sides, this coin is a virtual match to the predominant colors on the 1870 No LCW 50 Cents, an attractive proposition that enhances the desirability of the same bidder acquiring both pieces. While we cannot be certain, it appears likely that both coins resided for a long period in an old-time collection, where they developed similar coloration. With a bold strike and only a few scattered, minor contact marks, this Gem coin represents another remarkable opportunity in this string of landmark Canadian coins.
*From the Canadiana Collection*
Estimate: $50,000-$70,000  Starting Bid: $25,000

## Milestone Gem 1871 Victoria 50 Cents MS65

**20279 Victoria 50 Cents 1871,** KM6, MS65 PCGS, Ex: Pittman-Grossman. Although it was less than half of the 1870 combined mintage for the No LCW and With LCW 50 Cents, the 1871's mintage of 200,000 pieces was nonetheless the largest through the remainder of the Victoria series that ended in 1901. Such low production figures perhaps give a good indication of how incredibly challenging a series the Victoria half dollars are. Examples of the 1871 are scarce in all grades, and extremely rare in the higher Mint State levels. The cataloging of this coin in the Pittman Collection (David Akers, 8/1999, lot 2362) is still so completely pertinent today that we cannot resist quoting it *verbatim*:

**"50 Cents, 1871. Gem Uncirculated.** An absolutely magnificent coin that is not only the finest 1871 50 Cent piece known, but also one of the finest Victoria 50 Cent pieces of any date in existence. It is one of the greatest coins in the entire Pittman Collection of Canadian coins. The coin is sharply struck with superb quality, lustrous, semi-prooflike surfaces and beautiful, medium multi-colored toning, a gorgeous blend of russet, violet and blue with deeper shades at the borders. There are only a few microscopic marks hidden under the toning and the overall eye appeal of the piece is simply stunning. Whenever this coin has been displayed by as at various coin shows over the past several years, it has always been one of the most admired and talked about coins in our display. Purchased by [John Jay Pittman] as part of an 1871 mint set (the other denominations were offered earlier in this sale) from a Jim Charlton auction in November 1953 for $54.

*"All Victoria 50 Cent issues are rare in mint state, and most such pieces are only of minimal Uncirculated quality. At the Choice Uncirculated level, any Victoria 50 Cent piece is a major rarity and the number of true Gems known is extremely small. (For many issues, no Gems are known or at most one or two.) The 1871 is a very scarce, if not rare, date in grades above Extremely Fine, and although a few average quality Uncirculated examples are known, this piece is far and away the finest known and the only true Gem. It is a remarkable and exciting coin that everyone interested in Canadian coins should examine closely just for the sheer pleasure of seeing such a magnificent Victoria 50 Cent piece. A gorgeous Gem example of the famous 1921 is offered a little later in this sale, but in this condition the 1871 is significantly more rare."*

Those words ring as true today as they did when written a decade ago, and this splendid coin, whose appearance is unchanged, remains the lone Gem example certified at PCGS (7/09). It is equally true that the 1921 half dollar, long famed as the "King of Canadian Coins" (and an example of which is also in the present sale) has five pieces certified in MS65 or finer at PCGS—specifically, two each in MS65 and MS66, and one in MS67.

With an unparalleled desirability and unassailable pedigree, this coin should prove to be among the most outstanding performers in this milestone collection.
*From the Canadiana Collection*
Estimate: $90,000-$120,000  Starting Bid: $45,000

## Distinguished 1871-H Victoria 50 Cents MS67

**20280 Victoria 50 Cents 1871-H,** KM6, MS67 PCGS, Ex: Brown-Grossman. With only 45,000 pieces coined, the 1871-H Victoria 50 Cents, the first Heaton production, has the lowest mintage among the early-series issues. The low original production not-withstanding, this truly phenomenal Superb Gem coin has the dual distinction of being *not only the single finest graded of the issue by three grade points, it is also the single finest PCGS-certified example of the entire Victoria 50 Cents type* (7/09). Like most of the coins in this remarkable collection, this piece offers original old-time patina, here in shades of lilac and violet, with accents of blue on the obverse, while the reverse adds splashes of vivid amber-gold near the rims. The surfaces are incredibly smooth, as expected of the grade. Although this piece is not a Specimen coin, it clearly is a first strike from fresh dies—possibly a presentation piece to mark the beginning of the Heaton production?—and a coin that has been lovingly and carefully preserved ever since its production in Birmingham, England, nearly a century and a half ago. There are essentially no distractions, or even remote signs of contact, on either side, and we cannot overstate the tremendous eye appeal this piece will generate in the eyes of each and every viewer. For pedigree purposes, we note a small, curving lintmark or strike-through on the Queen's cheek, as made.

By way of comparison, two of the most notable Canadian collections in recent decades, the Belzberg and Pittman collections, had examples of substantially lower quality. The Belzberg coin (Heritage, 1/2003, lot 15473) was an MS63 (with only three certified finer at PCGS, including this piece) and quite rare as such; the Pittman Collection offered two examples, one XF and one VF (Akers, 8/1998, lots 2363 and 2364). Another distinguished coin in this noteworthy assemblage whose importance simply cannot be overstated.

*From the Canadiana Collection*
Estimate: $125,000-$175,000  Starting Bid: $62,500

## Incredible MS66 1872-H 50 Cents

**20281  Victoria 50 Cents 1872-H,** KM6, MS66 PCGS, Ex: Bandera-Campbell-Grossman. The last Victoria 50 Cents issue struck until the 1881-H coinage, as well as only the second series emission from the Heaton Mint. The mintage was 80,000 coins. The 1870 With LCW and the 1872-H issues are unusual in that they show more certified Mint State survivors at PCGS than other contemporaneous issues, some of which have only a couple to a half-dozen Mint State examples in all grade levels combined. The celebrated 1890H, for example, has two MS64 pieces at PCGS, and none others in Mint State. Even for the 1872-H, however, most of the Mint State examples cluster in the lower levels, from MS60 to MS64. The present splendid Premium Gem is the single finest certified of this issue at PCGS by two full grade points, and it is incredibly rare and desirable as such (7/09). Glints of lilac and ice-blue dominate the obverse, while the reverse offers somewhat more intense shades of amber, russet, and pinkish-purple.

A word about patina: Most of the Victoria 50 Cents in this remarkable collection show attractive, original patina that leads us to believe that at least some of them once resided in mint sets (in the case of the Pittman 1871, we know this to be the case). Whether they were once in mint sets is, however, somewhat beside the point: What matters is that they have been lovingly well preserved and never "fooled with" in a misguided attempt at "improvement." This is a case where brilliant is definitely *not* better, and many (or perhaps most) numismatists will prize their wonderfully colorful appearance.
*From the Canadiana Collection*
Estimate: $65,000-$80,000  Starting Bid: $32,500

**20282** **Victoria 50 Cents 1872-H,** KM6, Specimen 64 PCGS. The Province of Canada (1841-1867) issued no half dollars, so the first coins of this denomination were struck only in 1870, by the newly formed Dominion of Canada. An unknown number of Specimen 1872-H halves were minted, but based on their rarity today we know that it must have been a very small emission. PCGS has certified only three pieces in all grades (7/09).

This piece has an attractive ring of yellow-orange toning around the periphery, with a mix of gold, blue, red, and violet in the centers. The fields exhibit eye-catching reflectivity, which complements the powerfully struck design elements. Careful examination under a glass reveals just a couple of trivial contact marks. An outstanding Specimen issue.
*From the Canadiana Collection*
Estimate: $15,000-$20,000   Starting Bid: $7,500

## Coveted 1872-H Inverted A for V 50 Cents

20283 **Victoria 50 Cents 1872-H Inverted A for V in VICTORIA,** KM6, MS64 PCGS, Ex: Remick. Variously known as the A Over V, A/V, or Inverted A variety, this is a famous die-engraving blunder that makes the Queen's name appear to be AICTORIA, but with the first A upside-down. It perhaps speaks volumes to note that, for all issues in the Victoria 50 Cents series, PCGS has certified a skimpy total of only 137 pieces in all Mint State grades, a figure that undoubtedly includes numerous duplications. The 1872-H Inverted A is a variety that is elusive in any grade, and the present example is the single finest PCGS has certified (7/09). In point of fact, that service has graded only one other Mint State example an MS62.

This near-Gem coin offers original pinkish-purple patina on both sides, with dollops of sky-blue near the rims on both sides. The extra crossbar of the inverted A that begins the Queen's name is bold, and indeed the strike is uniformly crisp, save for minor softness on some of the hair high points. A few scattered marks are well hidden in the toning and of little consequence, as are some parallel planchet striations noted on the lower reverse. Most collectors can never hope to own an Uncirculated example and must settle for a circulated coin. One spirited bidder, however, can make this prize the centerpiece of a grand collection. As with so many of the coins offered in this remarkable assembly, it can be an interminable wait before a comparable example appears —if ever—in the marketplace.
*From the Canadiana Collection*
Estimate: $150,000-$200,000  Starting Bid: $75,000

## Exceptional 1881-H Victoria 50 Cents MS65

**20284  Victoria 50 Cents 1881-H**, KM6, MS65 PCGS, Ex: Alston-Grossman. The 1881-H issue was minted to the extent of 150,000 coins and is the most generally available of the early Heaton Mint issues, while still scarce in XF and rare in Mint State. The 1881-H features a somewhat different obverse (H3) that, according to the *Charlton Catalogue,* shows a "large space between crudely formed bow and ribbon at the nape of the neck." That anomaly and the generally poor workmanship of the dies have led to some speculation that this issue was struck after the date stamped.

The present example is exceptional in that regard, and it is the single finest certified and only Gem known to PCGS (7/09). Consistent tones of violet occupy both sides, and there are few significant contact marks. A small extra blob of metal is noted inside the G of REGINA, and the strike, while pleasing overall, is somewhat blunt on the venation of the lower reverse leaves—still a remarkable Gem and an incredibly elusive coin, but one that does seem to adhere to a somewhat lower production standard than the earlier Heaton Mint issues.

*From the Canadiana Collection*
Estimate: $50,000-$70,000  Starting Bid: $25,000

## Desirable 1888 Victoria 50 Cents MS63

**20285  Victoria 50 Cents 1888 Obverse 3,** KM6, MS63 PCGS, Ex: Alston-Grossman. The 1888 Victoria 50 Cents has a recorded mintage of 60,000 coins, divided between the H2 and H3 obverses, with the H2 somewhat more elusive. This is an interesting issue that perhaps requires reassessment: One notes that this date, of all the Victoria 50 Cents, has the lowest-graded examples as the finest in Mint State, at MS63. While the incredibly rare 1890H has two Mint State pieces, both in MS64, the 1888 shows 10 Mint State pieces at PCGS, with four MS63 the finest, including the present coin (7/09).

This is the H3 obverse as Charlton outlines, with a larger space between the ribbon and bow. Original pinkish-violet toning covers both sides, A few light ticks on the Queen's cheek and the obverse fields seemingly account for the grade, but this is still a coin of notable quality overall, tied for finest at PCGS.
*From the Canadiana Collection*
Estimate: $20,000-$30,000  Starting Bid: $10,000

## Unforgettable Key 1890-H Victoria 50 Cents

**20286  Victoria 50 Cents 1890H,** KM6, MS64 PCGS, Ex: Alston-Grossman. Now we come to another marvelous prize, one of the most coveted issues in Canadian numismatics. The 1890H is the rarest entry in the incredibly difficult Victoria 50 Cents series, with a mintage of only 20,000 coins. The 1890H is an elusive coin in any grade, and collectors eagerly seek examples when they appear infrequently in the marketplace. Even circulated examples are surprisingly elusive; most grade no better than VF or thereabouts.

The present near-Gem is one of only two Mint State examples known, both survivors of the renowned Heaton Hoard discovered in 1974-75 and long since dispersed to collectors, for the most part. It is only due to the existence of that hoard that *any* Mint State survivors of this issue are known. The Belzberg Collection example was an AU55, as was the Pittman Collection coin, and the Norweb Collection managed only a respectable XF45 piece.

The surfaces on this piece are lustrous silver-white, with little trace of color and few distractions of any sort, leading us to believe this piece could easily have been graded finer. For pedigree purposes we note a small nick on the Queen's neck, and some raised die lines on the reverse that run from the bottom right of the crown to the 0 in the date. Simply a splendid coin, one of unforgettable quality and a highlight of this memorable collection.
*From the Canadiana Collection*
Estimate: $175,000-$225,000  Starting Bid: $87,500

## Alluring Prooflike 1892 Victoria 50 Cents

**20287 Victoria 50 Cents 1892, Obverse 4,** KM6, MS65 PCGS, Ex: Robins-Belzberg. While not as celebrated as the 1890H, judging by the certified population at PCGS it is equally as rare (if perhaps the subject of less demand), since this Gem is the finer of the precisely two examples in Mint State at that service; the other coin is an MS64 (7/09).

The late-series Victoria 50 Cents issues were produced sporadically, at best. A gap of nearly a decade intervenes between the 1872-H and 1881-H issues, after which no coins were made again until 1888. Two more years passed between the 1888 and 1890H, then two more before the 1892 entry. Although the production of the 1892 was a relatively plentiful (for the series) 151,000 coins, it appears that most examples entered circulation directly. The average grade of the 39 coins certified at PCGS—presumably the high end of the total population—is only a bit over XF40.

As mentioned, this is the only Gem of the issue graded at PCGS, and the finer of the only two Mint State pieces that service has seen. This piece's most notable hallmark is gorgeous, fully prooflike surfaces on both sides, which has caused some authorities to question if this might be a Specimen striking. The mirrored surfaces are a marvelous complement to the near-pristine fields, the full strike, and the prevailing lilac-pink patina. This is another coin that we feel could have graded higher, as there are precious few signs of contact on either side, and they are all minor at best. For pedigree purposes we note a tiny, dotlike indentation on the reverse, just to the right of the bow ribbon. Despite a single small mark on the cheek, the Queen's cheek and neck elsewhere are exceptionally clean, adding further to the immense allure.
*From the Canadiana Collection*
Estimate: $65,000-$80,000  Starting Bid: $32,500

## Deeply Toned Gem 1894 50 Cents—Single Finest at PCGS

20288 **Victoria 50 Cents 1894,** KM6, MS65 PCGS. This late-series issue had a miserly mintage of only 29,036 pieces according to Charlton, the second-lowest of the entire series behind the vaunted 1890H issue. There are actually *fewer* examples of the 189 certified in circulated grades at PCGS than of the 1890H, although in Mint State the relations are reversed; that is, there are a few more Mint State examples graded of the 1894 than of the 1890H. (We note that the PCGS-certified population is not necessarily representative of the entire population.)

In any case, the present Gem is the finest and only example of the issue in MS65 that PCGS has certified (7/09). The obverse boasts an unusual but strictly original combination of intense sky-blue coloration that blends into pink and violet, with some patches of silver-white remaining. The reverse takes a more traditional approach, with hues of lilac melding into pinkish-gray. A few wispy marks appear in the reverse fields, as do a few insignificant signs of contact on the obverse that are well blended into the deep patina. The strike is uniformly bold throughout, lending further appeal to this rare and desirable coin.
*From the Canadiana Collection*
Estimate: $60,000-$80,000  Starting Bid: $30,000

## Elusive 1898 Victoria 50 Cents MS65

**20289  Victoria 50 Cents 1898,** KM6, MS65 PCGS, Ex: Grossman. The 1898 Victoria 50 Cents was issued after a four-year hiatus since the 1894 production, and the mintage of the 1898 was nearly four times as large as the skimpy 1894—100,000 coins for 1898, versus 29,000 and change for the 1894. Nonetheless, while PCGS has certified a few more examples of the 1898 in circulated grades, for statistical purposes both issues are equally rare in Mint State. As with the 1894 offered here, this is also the sole and finest certified 1898 half dollar at PCGS (7/09), further testament to its elusiveness.

Both sides of this coin show original toning in shades of pastel lilac, ceding to glints of blue near the rims. A few tiny marks appear on Victoria's cheek, with little evidence of contact elsewhere. The bold strike is just short of full, with detailed venation on the leaves and good articulation in the crowns on both sides. The Belzberg example was an MS62, formerly in the Norweb Collection.
*From the Canadiana Collection*
Estimate: $65,000-$80,000  Starting Bid: $32,500

**20290  Victoria 50 Cents 1899,** KM6, MS62 PCGS. The *Royal Mint Report* listed a mintage of 53,427 pieces, with a net of 50,000 "good coins." It contained an obvious typographical error when it said that two obverse and zero reverse dies were used. Based on the number of coins struck, it is more likely that a single pair of dies was employed.

Nearly all 50 Cents pieces of this era saw extensive circulation, and the 1899 is a significant condition rarity in AU and higher grades. The Norweb coin, which PCGS graded AU58, was described as "exceedingly rare at this grade level." As of this writing (7/09), PCGS has graded only three Mint State coins (all MS62).

Pale gray patina covers most of each side, with occasional accents of light gold in the periphery. Soft luster is seen in the margins. The strike is nearly full, and there are no significant marks. The specialist should not miss this important opportunity.
*From the Canadiana Collection*
Estimate: $12,000-$15,000   Starting Bid: $6,000

## Esteemed MS65 1900 Victoria 50 Cents

**20291** **Victoria 50 Cents 1900,** KM6, MS65 PCGS. The 1900 Victoria 50 Cents is the penultimate issue in the series, with a relatively generous mintage of 118,000 coins. The issue is nonetheless a rarity both in circulated grades and Mint State, even though there are a few more Uncirculated examples certified at PCGS than many of the earlier issues. Although that service has graded an even half-dozen pieces in MS64, the present Gem is the only one so graded, and there are none finer (7/09).

Both sides offer marvelous eye appeal. The original patina shows pinkish-gold predominating on the obverse with glints of ivory, while the reverse boasts a deeper palette with hues of russet and cinnamon. The Queen's cheek in particular and the surfaces throughout are essentially devoid of any mentionable contact. The full strike, pristine surfaces, and original toning add up to an estimable presentation on this finest certified example of the issue. Another prize for the aficionados of this difficult but rewarding Canadian series.
*From the Canadiana Collection*
Estimate: $60,000-$80,000  Starting Bid: $30,000

## High-End Near-Gem 1901 Victoria 50 Cents

**20292  Victoria 50 Cents 1901,** KM6, MS64 PCGS, Ex: Alston-Grossman. It is practically a truism in numismatics that the collecting public is more likely to save issues of a new design than the last year of an old design. The death of Queen Victoria on January 22, 1901, after a reign of nearly 64 years—the longest in British history—brought an end to the Victoria 50 Cents series, of course, although the final-year issue was a moderate production of 80,000 coins. Considering that her death occurred so early in the year and that her subjects in England and the colonies might have thought to save examples commemorating her reign, the issue is mystifyingly scarce in Mint State, a level at which PCGS has certified only seven pieces.

The present near-Gem is one of four so certified, with a single Gem finer (7/09). This piece has pinkish-gray centers that cede to glimpses of amber-gold near the rims, with premium eye appeal and a bold strike. A few tiny ticks on the Queen's cheek and jaw are minor but may have precluded an even finer grade. The reverse shows a single mark between the date and CENTS, likewise scarcely worthy of mention. A marvelous, high-end coin for the grade, and a wonderful representative of the type for last-year collectors.
*From the Canadiana Collection*
Estimate: $20,000-$30,000  Starting Bid: $10,000

**20293  Edward VII 50 Cents 1902,** KM12, MS66 PCGS. After the long reign of his mother, Queen Victoria, Edward VII assumed the throne in 1901 upon her passing and ruled for less than a decade before his own death in 1910, at age 68. The 1902 Edward VII 50 Cents is the first of his reign, produced to the extent of 120,000 coins. The dies were designed by G.W. DeSaulles, whose initials appear below the bust truncation. While there are more Uncirculated examples certified at PCGS of the 1902 than many of the Victoria issues, Gem coins are nonetheless quite scarce, and this Premium Gem is the sole finest of the issue certified at that service (7/09).

This splendid coin has a silver-white obverse center tinged with pinkish-gold at the rims. The details of the King's beard are well produced, although it and the lower crown details on the obverse are, as a rule, the least definitive parts of the design. The reverse displays deeper coloration, with lilac-pink in the center and violet at the margin. Signs of contact are few and far between. An incredibly eye-appealing example of this first-year Edward VII issue.
*From the Canadiana Collection*
Estimate: $17,500-$22,500   Starting Bid: $8,750

## Astounding MS66 1903-H 50 Cents—Tied for Finest at PCGS

20294 **Edward VII 50 Cents 1903-H,** KM12, MS66 PCGS. The only Heaton Mint issue of the Edward VII run, the 1903-H was produced to the extent of 140,000 coins, nominal within the series context. Of the 18 Uncirculated examples in all grades at PCGS, this piece is tied for finest known with one other example (7/09).

The relief on the Edward VII coins is high in relation to the rim; consequently, it is difficult to find coins with no rub or contact on the King's beard, in particular. The Heaton coins are also poorly struck compared to Royal Mint pieces of the same era. While this piece shows strictly no trace of rub, there is little detail on the King's beard or the lower crown details. More than offsetting, however, are the marvelously original surfaces, with silver-white, pinkish-gold, and ice- and steel-blue competing for territory on both sides. The luster is generous, and there are few visible signs of contact. An appealing example of this difficult issue .Sandy Campbell refers to this coin as the "Monster of Edward Halves".
*From the Canadiana Collection*
Estimate: $50,000-$70,000  Starting Bid: $25,000

## Remarkable 1904 50 Cents MS65

**20295** **Edward VII 50 Cents 1904,** KM12, MS65 PCGS. The 1904 and 1905 are the low-water marks in the Edward VII 50 Cents series, with production of 60,000 and 40,000 coins, respectively. Both are elusive even in circulated grades and quite scarce in Mint State. Cementing the rarity of this 1904 example is its status as the only Gem of the issue certified at PCGS, with none finer (7/09).

The coloration on both sides is a consistent lilac-pink, although glints of copper-gold and ice-blue are discernible at the extreme rims. The strike is well executed, but due to the design some weakness is still noted on the King's hair and beard. A few ticks appear in the central reverse, without which this piece might have achieved an even finer grade. Nonetheless a coin of remarkable quality and rarity.

*From the Canadiana Collection*
Estimate: $20,000-$30,000 Starting Bid: $10,000

**20296** **Edward VII 50 Cents 1906,** KM12, MS64 PCGS. As with almost all of the Edward VII half dollars, the 1906 is scarce in Mint State and rare in middle Uncirculated grades. Lovely blue and purple patina graces the margins, while the centers have rose-gold and steel-blue accents. The satiny surfaces have no marks of any significance. A crisply struck and attractive piece. PCGS Population: 6 in 64, 1 finer (7/09).
*From the Canadiana Collection*
Estimate: $6,500-$8,500   Starting Bid: $3,250

**20297** **Edward VII 50 Cents 1907,** KM12, MS65 PCGS. The 1907 is seldom seen in any Mint State grade, let alone Gem. This attractive Gem would be hard—if even possible—to match, even after years of diligent searching. PCGS has certified only four MS65 examples, with none finer (7/09).

Appealing violet toning dominates the margins; deep red, hazel, silver-gray and light blue occur elsewhere. Both sides appear nearly pristine, with only a few tiny marks seen under magnification. The strike is razor-sharp, save for a touch of softness on the bust high points. An excellent example of this conditionally rare issue.
*From the Canadiana Collection*
Estimate: $10,000-$12,000   Starting Bid: $5,000

**20298  Edward VII 50 Cents 1908,** KM12, MS65 PCGS. Although its diminutive mintage of 128,119 coins would suggest otherwise, the 1908 is one of the more available Edward VII 50 Cents in Mint State. Perhaps the relatively small emission caused people to save the 1908. This, however, does not mean that it is a common issue, and it is available only when compared to other Edward VII halves. In MS65 PCGS has certified a mere five examples, with two finer (7/09).

Mottled lilac, blue, reddish-gold, and silver-gray patina embraces both sides of this well-preserved Gem. There are just a few nearly microscopic handling marks. The strike is almost full, and glittering satiny luster radiates from the fields. A marvelous representative.
*From the Canadiana Collection*
Estimate: $7,000-$10,000   Starting Bid: $3,500

**20299  Edward VII 50 Cents 1909,** KM12, MS64 PCGS. The 1909 is a major condition rarity in the Edward VII 50 Cents series. While the 1904 and 1905 are more challenging, they had significantly lower mintages and are scarcer in all grades. In contrast, the 1909 is easily located in circulated condition, but its numbers drop precipitously in high grades. PCGS has certified only three MS64 examples and just two pieces finer (7/09).

Attractive sky-blue and rose-red patina in the centers yields to golden-brown along the rims. Sparkling satiny luster shines throughout the colorful surfaces. The details are exquisitely defined, and there are just a few minuscule marks, as typical for the grade. This piece boasts terrific eye appeal.
*From the Canadiana Collection*
Estimate: $12,000-$15,000   Starting Bid: $6,000

## Lustrous Gem Edward VII 1910 50 Cents

**20300** **Edward VII 50 Cents 1910,** KM12, MS65 PCGS, Ex: Norweb-Mason. Victorian Leaves. Edward VII died on May 6, 1910, after a reign of less than a decade. The last-year 1910 issue is by far the most plentiful of the entire series, produced to the extent of nearly 650,000 coins. This mintage is divided between the Victorian and Edwardian Leaves reverses, the latter the result of a modified reverse design to suit the Royal Canadian Mint in Ottawa.

This example is unsurprisingly of the Victorian Leaves variety, as the Edwardian Leaves type has but two examples certified in Mint State at PCGS, one in MS62, one in MS64. The present Gem is one of two Victorian Leaves at that service, and there are two finer, both MS66 (7/09). The pinkish-gold centers on both sides of this delightful piece blend into jade and ice-blue near the obverse rims, and into ivory, copper-russet, and grayish-blue at the reverse margins. There are no significant contact marks. Bountiful luster completes an attractive and eye-appealing package.
*From the Canadiana Collection*
Estimate: $30,000-$40,000  Starting Bid: $15,000

**20301  Edward VII 50 Cents 1910 Edwardian Leaves,** KM12a, MS64 PCGS. In 1910 W.H.J. Blakemore modified the reverse to improve the quality of the coins. Several leaves were made slightly smaller, the cross atop the crown was changed, and the rims were widened. This variety, termed Edwardian Leaves Reverse by collectors, is rare. PCGS has graded only 11 coins in all grades and just two pieces (MS62 and the present coin) in Mint State (7/09). This piece is by far the finest certified and would make an excellent addition to an advanced collection.

Variegated pale purple, silver-gray, blue, and tan toning envelops both sides. Flashy luster shines throughout the nearly perfect surfaces. A few light marks are nearly imperceptible beneath the delightful toning.
*From the Canadiana Collection*
Estimate: $7,000-$10,000   Starting Bid: $3,500

**20302  George V 50 Cents 1911,** KM19, MS65 PCGS. The first-year George V coins feature the "Godless" obverse, which lacks the abbreviation DEI GRA (for DEI GRATIA, by the Grace of God). The 1911 is one of the more challenging George V 50 Cents issues in Uncirculated grades. It very rare in MS65, with just three pieces so graded by PCGS (7/09).

The present coin has layers of rose-gold, light green, blue, violet toning on the top and bottom of the obverse, with occasional wafts of color in the mostly untoned middle region. The reverse is completely covered with deep purple and red patina. Shimmering satiny luster drapes the obverse, while the reverse has slightly subdued reflectivity. An outstanding representative of this interesting type.
*From the Canadiana Collection*
Estimate: $10,000-$12,000   Starting Bid: $5,000

**20303** **George V 50 Cents 1912,** KM25, MS66 PCGS, Ex: Cornwell. The lone finest survivor known to PCGS (7/09), with all the eye appeal a collector could want. Luminous peach and blue hues mingle throughout, and the boldly impressed portrait is surrounded by fields that offer subtle yet exquisite luster. The few marks present are trivial. In all respects, a wonderful representative of this popular early George V issue, the first to show the revised legend around the portrait that added DEI GRA to a design that had been decried as "Godless."
*From the Canadiana Collection*
Estimate: $15,000-$20,000   Starting Bid: $7,500

**20304** **George V 50 Cents 1913,** KM25, MS65 PCGS, Ex: Alston. Among the George V 50 Cents coins, the 1914 is easily the most challenging to acquire, particularly in XF and better grades. Aside from the 1914, however, the date that is the greatest condition rarity in Mint State is actually the 1913. This Gem is tied with two others for finest certified by PCGS (7/09), and the date's representation in this collection as an MS65, appearing alongside so many MS66 and even MS67 coins of a similar vintage, reinforces how conditionally elusive it is. Rich olive, slate-blue, and green-gold peripheral bands on each side frame minimally toned centers that are brightly lustrous. This sharply struck coin is carefully preserved and beautiful in all respects.
*From the Canadiana Collection*
Estimate: $12,500-$17,500   Starting Bid: $6,250

## The Norweb 1914 Canada 50 Cents MS66

**20305  George V 50 Cents 1914,** KM25, MS66 PCGS, Ex: Norweb. In November 1996, when this piece was offered as part of the Norweb Collection of Canadian and Provincial Coins, it was graded MS65 by PCGS; the currently assigned grade of MS66, though less conservative, is well-deserved. It is also the only MS66 grade awarded by PCGS to an example of the issue (7/09).

Green-gold and blue-gray toning dominates each side, though accents across a spectrum of pink are also visible. The strike is strong, and the surfaces are smooth and lustrous. The cataloger for this piece at its appearance in the Norweb auction noted: "In Mint State, this gem eclipses in rarity the far more famous 1921." In the PCGS *Population Report*, this holds true today, with eight Mint State 1914 coins to 11 certified as such of the 1921. It is important to remember, however, that this coin's importance and beauty are not found solely in comparisons, and that it is just as impressive when evaluated on its own merits.
*From the Canadiana Collection*
Estimate: $45,000-$60,000  Starting Bid: $22,500

**20306**   **George V 50 Cents 1916,** KM25, MS65 PCGS. The 1916 is extremely difficult to locate above low Mint State grades. The present coin is the finest example certified by PCGS (7/09). At first glance this piece appears entirely silver-gray, but a closer look reveals pleasing hints of gold and rose. Captivating satiny luster embraces the lightly abraded surfaces. The strike is nearly full. Several thin die cracks are visible on each side. An excellent piece for the specialist.
*From the Canadiana Collection*
Estimate: $6,000-$8,000   Starting Bid: $3,000

**20307**   **George V 50 Cents 1917,** KM25, MS66 PCGS. The 1917 is surprisingly elusive in high Mint State grades, despite its mintage of 752,213 pieces. The Norweb piece (Bowers and Merena, 11/1996, lot 416) was only graded MS64 by PCGS, and the catalog noted that the 1917 is "seldom seen in grades even approaching this." PCGS has certified only four MS66 examples, with none finer (7/09). Splendid orange-gold patina encircles the pale gray centers of this lustrous Premium Gem. The strike is nearly full. A few faint abrasions do not affect the impressive eye appeal.
*From the Canadiana Collection*
Estimate: $4,500-$6,000   Starting Bid: $2,250

**20308  George V 50 Cents 1918,** KM25, MS65 PCGS. Splashes of golden-brown patina in the margins blends well with the silver-gray over the centers. The splendid satiny sheen is unaffected by a few minor luster grazes in the fields. The strike is nearly full, and the eye appeal is great. The 1918 is rare above Choice Mint State. PCGS has certified only five MS65 examples and just one piece finer (7/09).
*From the Canadiana Collection*
Estimate: $3,500-$5,000   Starting Bid: $1,750

**20309  George V 50 Cents 1919,** KM25, MS67 PCGS. The final year struck with a sterling (.925) fineness. The 1919 is probably the easiest George V half dollar to locate in most grades, but it becomes rare above Choice Mint State. PCGS has graded only four pieces in MS65, one in 66, and one—the present coin and finest certified—in MS67 (7/09). A lovely ring of cobalt-blue and violet toning yields to red and orange in the centers. Shimmering satiny luster radiates beneath the attractive patina. The surfaces appear nearly perfect without magnification, and the strike is razor-sharp.
*From the Canadiana Collection*
Estimate: $12,000-$15,000   Starting Bid: $6,000

**20310** **George V 50 Cents 1920 Narrow O,** KM25a, MS65 PCGS. The Narrow O is identified by the thin 0. The more available of the two varieties for the year, both of which are fairly scarce because a significant number were melted in 1929. Delightful violet, blue-green, and red-gold toning surrounds the lighter-colored centers. The satiny surfaces have only a few inconsequential abrasions. This is a terrific representative of the issue and type. PCGS Population for both varieties: 3 in 65, 2 finer (7/09).
*From the Canadiana Collection*
Estimate: $7,500-$10,000   Starting Bid: $3,750

**20311** **George V 50 Cents 1920 Wide O,** KM25a, MS65 PCGS. This variety is moderately scarcer than its Narrow O counterpart. A touch of hazel near the rims adds color to the nearly brilliant surfaces. This Gem boasts magnificent satiny luster throughout. Faint die striations appear on both sides. The strike is needle-sharp, and there are no significant marks. PCGS does not differentiate between Narrow and Wide O 1920 halves, but the population data indicates that both are rare at this level. PCGS Population for both varieties: 3 in 65, 2 finer (7/09).
*From the Canadiana Collection*
Estimate: $12,000-$15,000   Starting Bid: $6,000

## The 'King of Canadian Coins' - A Stunning 1921 50 Cents

**20312** **George V 50 Cents 1921,** KM25a, MS66 PCGS, Ex: Bass-Belzberg-Brown. At its previous appearance in the Belzberg Collection, auctioned by Heritage in January 2003, this example was graded MS65 by PCGS and also MS65 by ICCS. The issue has long been known as the "King of Canadian Coins," a rarity that saw only a few survivors escape the mint before the date's mass melting. As the *Charlton Catalogue* explains:

"This popular and very scarce coin was originally minted in considerable quantity. During the early and mid-1920s the demand for 50-cent pieces was very light; only 28,000 pieces were issued between 1921 and 1929. These are assumed to have been almost entirely 1920s. When a greater demand for this denomination arose later in 1929, the Master of the Ottawa Mint decided to melt the entire stock of 1920 and 1921 coins (amounting to some 480,392 pieces) and recoin the silver into 1929 coins. He took this decision because he feared that the public would suspect they were receiving counterfeits if a large quantity of coins with 'old' dates were issued. It is believed that the 75 or so 1921s that have survived came from Specimen sets sold to collectors, or from circulation strikes sold to Mint visitors."

Certainly, this example was well-kept from the time it was acquired. Both sides have powerful, slightly satiny luster that filters through rich green-gold and reddish-orange patina that shows copper and silver-gray accents. A shallow mark to the right of the last A in CANADA, in a hollow between two maple leaves, serves as a pedigree marker. A strong candidate for any Condition Census for the date.

*From the Canadiana Collection*

Estimate: $200,000-$250,000  Starting Bid: $100,000

20313 **George V 50 Cents 1929,** KM25a, MS65 PCGS. The 1929 is the first half dollar struck since 1921. Demand for silver coins dropped precipitously in the early part of the decade, and production was halted for several years. Pleasing violet and yellow-gold toning surrounds the gray obverse center, while the reverse has more color, with sky-blue and red accents. Both sides appear remarkably clean, and there is splendid satiny luster throughout. This sharply struck Gem is tied with six others at PCGS for finest certified (7/09).
*From the Canadiana Collection*
Estimate: $3,500-$5,000   Starting Bid: $1,750

20314 **George V 50 Cents 1931,** KM25a, MS67 PCGS, Ex: Alston. More than 200,000 1921-dated half dollars were produced, but most were melted late in the 1920s when the Master of the Mint made the large 1929 emission of 228,328 coins. The few dozen surviving 1921 half dollars are mostly from Specimen sets or business strikes sold to Mint visitors. After the 1929 production, no 1930-dated half dollars were produced, and the 1931 saw only 57,581 coins made. Not only is the 1931 a popular date due to its small mintage, but also because of its association with the famed 1921 issue. This piece is one of three MS67 pieces tied for the top spot at PCGS (7/09). The pristine surfaces are brilliant silver-white throughout, with just a hint of lilac coloration. The full strike is inimitable, and a finer coin is simply unimaginable.
*From the Canadiana Collection*
Estimate: $15,000-$20,000   Starting Bid: $7,500

## Famous Low-Mintage 1932 50 Cents MS65

20315 **George V 50 Cents 1932,** KM25a, MS65 PCGS. An astounding Gem that stands as finest certified by PCGS by two grade points (7/09). This result is curious, since in November 1996, the Norweb coin was graded MS64 by PCGS; there is no such entry in the current *PCGS Population Report.* The natural instinct is to think that perhaps this unprovenanced MS65 is the Norweb coin, since very few of the Norweb coins have gone *down* in grade level since then; however, plate-matching and the description reveal that the two coins are different. It is more likely that this is simply an extraordinary survivor of one of the most famous low-mintage dates in Canadian coinage.

This Gem is boldly impressed with remarkable luster that filters through rich silver-gray and green-gold toning. There are no individually mentionable abrasions or other flaws, and the eye appeal is strong. One of just 19,213 pieces struck and a distinctly rare date in any Mint State grade, much less a strong MS65.
*From the Canadiana Collection*
Estimate: $20,000-$30,000  Starting Bid: $10,000

**20316  George V 50 Cents 1934,** KM25a, MS66 PCGS. The 1934 has a low mintage of just under 40,000 coins. Mint State examples are scarce. A ring of violet and reddish-orange patina encircles the silver-gray centers of this appealing Premium Gem. Several pin-sized abrasions preclude a higher grade, but none merit specific mention. Shimmering satiny luster highlights the boldly struck details. PCGS has graded only three MS66 examples and just one piece (an MS67) finer (7/09).
*From the Canadiana Collection*
Estimate: $4,500-$6,500  Starting Bid: $2,250

**20317  George V 50 Cents 1936,** KM25a, MS66 PCGS, Ex: Belzberg. This is the final year with an Edwardian Leaves Reverse design. In our catalog of the Sid and Alicia Belzberg Collection of Canadian Coinage, we described this piece thusly:

"The obverse has a lustrous, golden toned center with slightly mottled gold, russet, and steel-blue peripheral toning. The reverse has incredible lavender patina with golden highlights. The strike is bold and only a few minute marks mar the near-perfect surfaces. This date has always been a popular type date and this coin is a perfect fit for either the type set or date set."

PCGS has certified seven examples at the MS66 level, with none finer (7/09).
*From the Canadiana Collection*
Estimate: $4,000-$6,000  Starting Bid: $2,000

**20318** **George VI 50 Cents 1937,** KM36, MS64 PCGS. Both sides of the half dollar were changed in 1937. The obverse featured a portrait of George VI, who was crowned on December 11, 1936. The Royal Mint took the opportunity to alter the reverse to sport a stylized, attractive Canadian coat of arms designed by George Edward Kruger-Gray. Captivating cartwheel luster radiates from the lightly abraded surfaces. Attractive light green, violet, red, and gold toning encircles the silver-gray centers. A sharply struck and appealing near-Gem. PCGS has graded seven pieces finer (7/09).
*From the Canadiana Collection*
Estimate: $100-$200  No Minimum Bid

**20319** **George VI 50 Cents 1938,** KM36, MS66 PCGS, Ex: Pittman. Speckled violet and deep red toning surrounds the silver-gray and frosty centers. The reverse appears pristine to the unaided eye, while the obverse has only a couple of pin-sized marks. Splendid satiny luster glistens throughout the fields. The 1938 50 Cents becomes rare in Gem condition. PCGS has certified only two MS66 examples, with none finer (7/09).
*From the Canadiana Collection*
Estimate: $7,500-$8,500   Starting Bid: $3,750

**20320** **George VI 50 Cents 1939,** KM36, MS65 PCGS. Vibrant teal, cobalt-blue, red, and gold patina envelops the periphery, while the centers are largely silver-gray. Flashy luster radiates beneath the attractive toning. The central reverse is a touch soft, but other details are powerfully impressed. A few small abrasions on George's cheek preclude an even higher grade. PCGS has graded only seven MS65 examples, none finer (7/09).
*From the Canadiana Collection*
Estimate: $2,000-$2,200 Starting Bid: $1,000

**20321** **George VI 50 Cents 1940,** KM36, MS65 PCGS. The 1940 is conditionally rare at the MS65 level, where PCGS reports just two such examples, with none finer (7/09). This resplendent Gem exhibits pleasing violet and red-orange toning around the brilliant interior. The strike is sharp, save for a touch of weakness on the centers. Scintillating satiny luster in the fields and lightly frosted devices enhance the eye appeal. The reverse is remarkably clean, while the obverse has only minor, grade-consistent abrasions.
*From the Canadiana Collection*
Estimate: $1,200-$1,500 Starting Bid: $600

**20322** **George VI 50 Cents 1941,** KM36, MS65 PCGS. Narrow Date, which is slightly more available than the Wide Date variety. Magnificent prooflike reflectivity shines from the well-preserved surfaces. There are just a few minuscule handling marks visible on the obverse, and the reverse is nearly perfect. Splashes of light red and lilac accent the perimeter, while the centers are brilliant. An outstanding, boldly struck Gem. PCGS Population for both varieties: 3 in 65, 1 finer (7/09).
*From the Canadiana Collection*
Estimate: $1,200-$1,500 Starting Bid: $600

**20323** **George VI 50 Cents 1942,** KM36, MS65 PCGS, Wide Date. This variety is scarcer than its Narrow Date counterpart, particularly in high grades. Red, orange, and violet patina accents the borders and contrasts against the untoned centers. The fields have an eye-catching semi-prooflike sheen, and the devices are lightly frosted. A hint of weakness is noted above the King's ear and the top right of the shield. For both varieties, PCGS has graded only four pieces at the MS65 level, with none finer (7/09).
*From the Canadiana Collection*
Estimate: $1,200-$1,500 Starting Bid: $600

**20324  George VI 50 Cents 1943 Far 3,** KM36, MS64 PCGS. Wide Date, per the *Charlton Catalogue* (2009). A hint of tan patina visits the margins, but for the most part this attractive near-Gem is bright silver-gray. Splendid semi-prooflike fields show moderate contrast against the frosted devices. The centers are a bit soft, as often seen, but details elsewhere are bold. A few wispy grazes do not dampen the impressive eye appeal. PCGS has certified only four examples finer (7/09).
*From the Canadiana Collection*
Estimate: $250-$450  No Minimum Bid

**20325  George VI 50 Cents 1944 Near 4,** KM36, MS65 PCGS. A vibrantly toned and highly lustrous Gem. The recesses in and around the bust of George VI are filled with attractive blue-green patina, while the high points exhibit intermingled red and gray toning. The perimeter boasts appealing violet and blue, with occasional light green accents. Delightful luster percolates beneath the deep patina. Inspection reveals only a few nearly imperceptible marks. The strike is sharp, save for a bit of softness on the centers. The 1944 is elusive at this lofty level. PCGS Population: 6 in 65, 2 finer (7/09).
*From the Canadiana Collection*
Estimate: $1,200-$1,500  Starting Bid: $600

**20326  George VI 50 Cents 1945,** KM36, MS64 PCGS. Deep red, violet, and blue toning encircles the brilliant centers. The fields exhibit tremendous reflectivity and show moderate contrast against the lightly frosted devices. This piece has a number of die striations on the obverse, particularly around the King's neck. The reverse is nearly perfect, while the obverse has only a few minor handling marks. It would be difficult to improve upon the impressive eye appeal of this attractively toned near-Gem. PCGS has certified only three examples finer (7/09).
*From the Canadiana Collection*
Estimate: $100-$300  No Minimum Bid

**20327  George VI 50 Cents 1946,** KM36, MS65 PCGS. Narrow Date, per Charlton (2009). The 1946 50 Cents is not rare in the absolute sense but becomes scarce above Select Mint State. This outstanding Gem boasts eye-catching prooflike fields and moderate cameo contrast. Attractive purple and golden patina coats the perimeter, with untoned, frosted centers. The left side of the crown and shield top are weakly struck, but the impression is sharp otherwise. A few light abrasions on the King's cheek do not distract. PCGS has certified only five MS65 examples, with none finer (7/09).
*From the Canadiana Collection*
Estimate: $3,000-$4,000  Starting Bid: $1,500

20328 **George VI 50 Cents 1946 Hoof Through 6,** KM36, MS62 PCGS. Charlton (2009) calls this variety Hoof through 6, Narrow Date. PCGS, for reasons unknown, refers to it simply as "Design." Although Charlton says that the hoof goes through the 6 in the date, the hoof appears to be outside the loop. In reality, the so-called "hoof" is a tiny die break connected to the rim by a thin die crack.

Hints of tan toning accent the perimeter, with an area of deeper patina around the 19 in the date. Scattered abrasions define the grade, none worthy of specific mention. Both sides show clash marks, particularly noticeable on the reverse. Numerous faint die striations appear in the obverse margins. The strike is sharp, save for some typical central softness. This variety is very rare in Mint State, and PCGS has certified only four such examples. Only one piece, an MS63, has been graded finer than this coin (7/09).
*From the Canadiana Collection*
Estimate: $2,000-$3,000   Starting Bid: $1,000

20329 **George VI 50 Cents 1947 Curved Left,** KM36, MS65 PCGS. Straight 7, Wide Date according to Charlton (2009). The 7 in the date is slightly repunched east, and the bottom is curved to the left. Deep battleship-gray, purple, and gold toning covers the obverse; the reverse shows blue, green, and red. The strike is nearly full. A rare issue above Select Mint State. PCGS Population: 2 in 65, 1 finer (7/09).
*From the Canadiana Collection*
Estimate: $3,000-$5,000   Starting Bid: $1,500

**20331** **George VI 50 Cents 1947 Curved Right 7,** KM36, Specimen 64 PCGS, Wide Date, according to Charlton (2009). In Specimen format this variety is believed to have had a mintage of a few dozen pieces, and it is slightly scarcer than its Straight 7 (also called Curved Left) counterpart. This brilliant near-Gem is powerfully lustrous and sharply struck. A few nearly microscopic blemishes and contact marks keep this piece from being absolutely flawless. PCGS Population: 5 in 64, 6 finer (7/09).
*From the Canadiana Collection*
Estimate: $1,500-$1,700   Starting Bid: $750

**20330** **George VI 50 Cents 1947 Curved Right 7,** KM36, MS65 PCGS, Narrow Date. The bottom of the 7 in the date curves slightly to the right. An attractively toned Gem with red, gold, violet, and blue patina, accented by silver-gray on the bust. The left side of the shield is a touch soft, but other details are sharp. A few minuscule marks blend well with the eye-catching patina. PCGS has certified just four MS65 examples, with none finer (7/09).
*From the Canadiana Collection*
Estimate: $4,000-$6,000   Starting Bid: $2,000

20332  **George VI 50 Cents 1947 Maple Leaf Curved Left 7,** KM36, MS66 PCGS. Charlton (2009) calls this the Straight 7 variety. The bottom of the 7 in the date is curved slightly to the left. A small maple leaf was added to the right of the date to indicate that these pieces were struck using outdated dies, which still had ET IND: IMP: (and Emperor of India) in the legend. Only 38,433 examples of both Maple Leaf varieties were struck, compared to 424,885 pieces for the regular 1947 halves.

Mottled gold, light blue, and lavender toning drapes both sides of this prooflike Premium Gem. The surfaces appear remarkably pristine to the unaided eye, and a loupe locates only a couple of wispy luster grazes. A sharply struck and attractive piece, the single finest certified by PCGS (7/09).
*From the Canadiana Collection*
Estimate: $4,000-$6,000   Starting Bid: $2,000

20333  **George VI 50 Cents 1947 Maple Leaf Curved Right 7,** KM36, MS61 PCGS. Both varieties of 1947 Maple Leaf halves are elusive, but the 1947 Curved (Right) 7 is by far the rarer. Uncirculated examples are virtually unheard of, and PCGS reports only two Mint State pieces (the present coin and an MS62) out of a total of just 23 coins in all grades (7/09). This variety is so rare in high grades that Charlton (2009) does not even list a value above XF. Collectors seldom have the chance to acquire even a circulated representative, and this Mint State piece represents an important opportunity for the serious collector.

This near-brilliant coin exhibits outstanding prooflike reflectivity, which is unaffected by scattered, light abrasions. Typical softness is limited to the King's hair, with a bold strike elsewhere. It may be years before another Mint State 1947 Curved Right Maple Leaf half is offered at auction.
*From the Canadiana Collection*
Estimate: $10,000-$12,000   Starting Bid: $5,000

**20334  George VI 50 Cents 1947 Maple Leaf Curved Right 7,** KM36, Specimen 64 PCGS. The bottom of the 7 in the date is curved to the right. The 1947 Maple Leaf, Curved 7 half is a significant rarity in business strike format, which places increased demand on Specimen issues. No Specimens of the Straight 7 (Curved Left 7) Maple Leaf variety were minted. The exact mintage of Specimen 1947 Maple Leaf Curved Right 7 50 Cents is unknown, but it is believed to have been very small.

Lovely light red patina covers most of both sides, with a touch of peripheral violet toning on the reverse. The deeply mirrored fields show only a faint hint of contact. The strike is razor-sharp, and the eye appeal is excellent. PCGS Population: 6 in 64, 11 finer (7/09).
*From the Canadiana Collection*
Estimate: $4,000-$6,000   Starting Bid: $2,000

**20335  George VI 50 Cents 1948,** KM45, MS65 PCGS. The 1948 50 Cents had a diminutive mintage of just 37,784 pieces, the lowest since 1932—probably because the requirement to remove ET IND IMP from the obverse delayed the production of new dies well into 1948 and forced the production of the 1947-dated Maple Leaf varieties. Pleasing violet and golden-brown patina encircles the silver-gray centers of the present piece. Captivating semi-prooflike reflectivity in the fields complements the boldly struck design elements. Several tiny abrasions are nearly imperceptible without magnification. PCGS has certified only two examples finer (7/09).
*From the Canadiana Collection*
Estimate: $2,000-$3,000   Starting Bid: $1,000

20336 **George VI 50 Cents 1949,** KM45, MS65 PCGS. Narrow Date, which is slightly scarcer than the Wide Date variety. Gold, lilac, and steel-blue accent the prooflike surfaces of this well-preserved Gem. A few minuscule contact marks account for the grade, but this sharp Gem is a terrific representation of the date and type. PCGS has certified five pieces finer (7/09).
*From the Canadiana Collection*
Estimate: $1,200-$1,500   Starting Bid: $600

20337 **George VI 50 Cents 1949 Hoof,** KM45, MS64 PCGS. Wide Date, as always for this variety. The hoof extends over the right side of the 9 in the date. This variety is scarce in all grades and rare in Mint State. PCGS reports just 16 examples for all grades. The present coin is tied with two others for finest certified (7/09). Splashes of tan and light blue accent the highly reflective surfaces. Several minor abrasions define the grade, but none merit specific mention. The strike is nearly full. A superior example of this seldom-seen variety.
*From the Canadiana Collection*
Estimate: $2,000-$3,000   Starting Bid: $1,000

**20338  George VI 50 Cents 1950 Full Design,** KM45, MS66 PCGS. All of the lines around the date are clearly defined. Although this variety is easily located in most grades, it becomes rare above Choice Mint State. PCGS has certified only two MS66 examples, with none finer (7/09). Dazzling prooflike reflectivity enhances this carefully preserved Premium Gem. The strike is nearly full, and there are only a couple of wispy luster grazes. Dappled orange and rose-red accent the margins of this lightly toned piece. A spectacular example of this popular variety.
*From the Canadiana Collection*
Estimate: $750-$1,000   Starting Bid: $375

**20339  George VI 50 Cents 1951,** KM45, MS66 PCGS, Narrow Date. The two varieties of the year appear to have had about equal mintages. PCGS does not differentiate between Narrow and Wide Dates. Impressive multicolored toning covers the prooflike surfaces of this remarkable Premium Gem. Pleasing blue and purple patina near the rims yields to yellow-gold, orange, red, and pale gray towards the centers. A few minor contact marks blend well with the vivid patina. The strike is bold. An attractive and conditionally rare representative. For both varieties, PCGS Population: 3 in 66, 0 finer (7/09).
*From the Canadiana Collection*
Estimate: $350-$550   Starting Bid: $175

**20340  George VI 50 Cents 1952,** KM45, MS66 PCGS, Narrow Date. This is the popular final issue of George VI's reign. Light toning over the centers yields to deeper violet, red, blue, and green around the margins. Eye-catching prooflike luster shines beneath the pleasing patina. The northwest quadrant of the shield is a trifle soft, but other details are sharply struck. A few pin-sized handling marks preclude an even higher grade. PCGS has certified only five MS66 examples (both varieties), with none finer (7/09).
*From the Canadiana Collection*
Estimate: $300-$500   Starting Bid: $150

**20341  George V Dollar 1935,** KM30, Specimen 68 PCGS, a lovely pinkish-gray example accented with blushes of teal-blue near the reverse rim and strong eye appeal throughout. In Specimen 68 this coin is one of three coins so graded at PCGS, and there are 13 finer (7/09). However, the Specimen issues of 1935 were produced in both matte and satin finishes, with the present piece one of the satin finish varieties—a distinction that PCGS does not make, but one that further reduces the certified populations of each when the differences are considered.

The 1935 George V Dollar was the first Canadian commemorative coin as well as its first circulating silver Dollar, minted to mark the 25th anniversary of the accession of George V. The obverse design, by Percy Metcalfe, makes the issue a one-year type, with the ANNO REGNI XXV phrase that concludes the peripheral inscription touting the Silver Jubilee. The reverse, by Emanuel Hahn, features the familiar canoe and "voyageur" design used through 1986. Both the Specimen 1935 and 1936 issues were formerly considered great rarities, but a few pieces released by a mint employee have made them more available than previously, while still quite elusive. George V died shortly after the Silver Jubilee on January 20, 1936, so it is likely that the 1936-dated coins were actually struck during the short, following reign of Edward VIII. An estimable Gem example of this popular and important first-year and one-year type.
*From the Canadiana Collection*
Estimate: $6,000-$8,000   Starting Bid: $3,000

**20343  George VI Dollar 1937,** KM37, Mirror Specimen 66 PCGS. The first of the silver Dollar issues of George VI, whose reign was precipitated by the abdication of Edward VIII in December 1936. Mirror Specimens of this issue are quite rare in Gem and finer grades. This is a brilliant silver-white piece with splendidly deep mirrors and wonderful eye appeal. PCGS has certified seven pieces in this grade, with a single Specimen 67 finer.
*From the Canadiana Collection*
Estimate: $1,500-$2,000   Starting Bid: $750

**20342  George V Dollar 1936,** KM31, Specimen 67 PCGS, Ex: Pittman-Belzberg-Brown. Although the insert says Belzberg, the Belzberg example was a Specimen 65 coin (Heritage, 1/2003, lot 15550). Marvelously patinated in shades of crystal-blue and lilac, with a couple of dashes of copper-gold adding a splendid accent to the Northern Lights at the reverse rims. A lovely example of the satin finish variant, far finer than the Belzberg coin which had a couple of small spots. Rare and desirable, especially in so fine a grade. PCGS has certified seven coins in this grade (with possible duplications) and none finer (8/09).This is the Belzberg/Pittman example from the 1936 dot set.
*From the Canadiana Collection*
Estimate: $15,000-$20,000   Starting Bid: $7,500

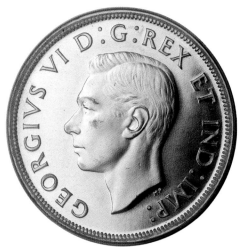

**20344**  **George VI Dollar 1939,** KM38, Mirror Specimen 67 PCGS, Ex: Pittman. A one-year type with the Royal Visit reverse. In 1939 as World War II loomed, King George VI and Queen Elizabeth (now known as the Queen Mother), began a month-long tour of the Dominion of Canada, the first by a reigning monarch. The Specimen commemorative silver Dollars are found with both matte and mirror finishes, of which the mirror version is far more elusive. This piece, one of the five finest at PCGS with the mirror finish, is brilliant silver-white, well mirrored, and highly attractive. A popular issue; the Latin inscription on the reverse, FIDE SUORUM REGNAT, translates to "He reigns by the faith of his people."
*From the Canadiana Collection*
Estimate: $2,750-$3,750   Starting Bid: $1,375

**20345**  **George VI Dollar 1939,** KM38, Matte Specimen 67 PCGS, the commemorative Royal Visit reverse, a one-year type. One of 20 Specimen 67 pieces tied for finest certified at PCGS of this more-available matte finish (7/09). On this piece the obverse has lilac and pink dominating, deepening into violet and indigo near the lower rim. The reverse has a crescent of bluish-gray, accented by pinks and purples.
*From the Canadiana Collection*
Estimate: $2,000-$4,000   Starting Bid: $1,000

**20346 George VI Dollar 1947 Blunt 7,** KM37, Specimen 64 PCGS. The Norweb catalog notes: "Both the Pointed 7 and Blunt 7 varieties are scimitar-shaped. The Blunt 7 really is not blunt at all but, rather, is truncated or abbreviated in its length." This variety is rarer in high grades than its Pointed 7 counterpart. This powerfully reflective near-Gem has just a touch of color around the margins. The strike is bold, and there are no marks of any consequence. PCGS has certified only 12 examples in all grades and just six pieces finer than the present coin (7/09).
*From the Canadiana Collection*
Estimate: $5,000-$7,000   Starting Bid: $2,500

**20347 George VI Dollar 1947 Pointed 7, Triple HP,** KM37, Specimen 67 PCGS, Ex: Alston. This variety is identified by the long point at the bottom of the 7 in the date. The exact number of Dollars struck in Specimen format is unknown, but it must have been quite low.

Deeply mirrored fields show moderate contrast against the lightly frosted devices. A small lint mark near the first L in DOLLAR is noted for future pedigree purposes. Hints of hazel and purple visit the rims, but the centers are virtually brilliant. This carefully preserved Superb Gem is nearly fully struck and has spectacular eye appeal. PCGS has only graded three pieces at the Specimen 67 level, with none finer (7/09).
*From the Canadiana Collection*
Estimate: $17,500-$22,500   Starting Bid: $8,750

**20348** **George VI Dollar 1948,** KM46, Specimen 66 PCGS, the key to the George VI series, with business strikes produced to the extent of only 18,780 pieces. The Belzberg example (Heritage, 1/2003, lot 15570) was an amazing MS66 coin. Only mirrored Specimens were produced of the 1948 (no matte or satin pieces). This is a brilliant coin, silver-white with radiant mirrors and wonderful eye appeal. PCGS has certified only three Specimen 67s finer (8/09).
*From the Canadiana Collection*
Estimate: $10,000-$12,000   Starting Bid: $5,000

**20349** **George VI Dollar 1950 Arnprior,** KM46, Specimen 66 PCGS, Ex: Alston-Wellington Collection. Very rare as a Specimen. Silver-white with just a bare tinge of pinkish-gold color. The Belzberg coin was a Specimen 65. Only five examples have been certified by PCGS as Specimen 66, and none finer (8/09).
*From the Canadiana Collection*
Estimate: $5,000-$7,000   Starting Bid: $2,500

**20350** **George VI Dollar 1951,** KM46, Specimen 64 PCGS, Short Water Lines. As with many Specimen issues of this era, the exact mintage is unknown, but the 1951 Dollar's distribution is estimated at several hundred pieces at most. A touch of hazel in the periphery enhances the mostly silver-gray surfaces. The deeply mirrored fields appear watery, and there only a few light hairlines. A sharply struck near-Gem. PCGS Population: 7 in 64, 21 finer (7/09).
*From the Canadiana Collection*
Estimate: $1,500-$2,000  Starting Bid: $750

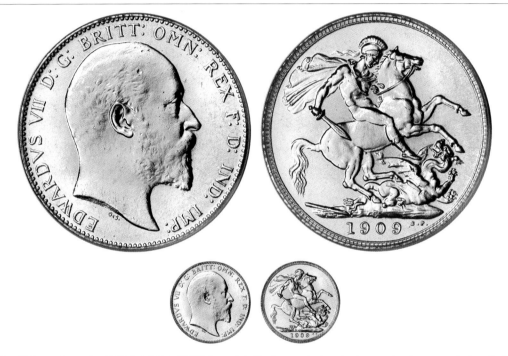

**20351** **Edward VII gold Sovereign 1909-C,** KM14, MS65 PCGS, bust right/St. George slaying the dragon, date in exergue below, Ex Campbell. There are lots of "commercial-grade" sovereigns around, both raw and certified, in the AU and lower Mint State grades, up to MS62 or so. However, in the upper reaches of Mint State, MS63 through MS67 or so, they are not only nearly unobtainable, they are also astoundingly beautiful when found with choice surfaces. The Ottawa Mint sovereigns (with mintmark C for Canada) are increasingly popular issues among many collectors, along with some other branch mint issues from India, Australia, and South Africa, the Victoria Jubilee sovereigns, and the Australian "shield backs" in general.

The Edward VII sovereigns are a study in contrasts: While the 1908-C sovereign is a Specimen-only issue produced to the extent of 636 pieces (according to Charlton, or 633 according to Michael A. Marsh in *The Gold Sovereign,* Jubilee edition), the 1909-C and 1910-C saw mintages in the low tens of thousands and today are considered R2, or "very rare," in the Marsh reference. In total contrast, the Edward VII sovereigns with the S, M, and P mintmarks (for Sydney, Melbourne, and Perth, Australia) are all considered quite common (or nearly so) and all produced in the millions of coins each. (One hastens to add that a large percentage of the sovereigns of any stripe were melted in one of several extinction events of the 1920s and 1930s, much as happened with most U.S. gold coinage of that era.)

The present 1909-C is one of only two Gems for the issue certified at PCGS, and there are none finer. This is a splendid piece with yellow-gold color at the margins and tinges of reddish-gold in the center. The strike is boldly impressed, and only a couple of dotlike contact marks appear on the King's upper brow, with one on the horse's shoulder. The devices elsewhere are remarkably pristine. An amazing coin, both in its quality and in its rarity. Expect runaway bidding on this piece and the other memorable sovereigns in this collection.
*From the Canadiana Collection*
Estimate: $15,000-$20,000  Starting Bid: $7,500

**20352  Edward VII gold Sovereign 1910-C,** KM14, MS65 PCGS, bust right/St. George slaying the dragon, date in exergue below, Ex: Cornwell. Another Ottawa Mint sovereign of this equally rare (to the 1909-C) issue, produced to the extent of 28,020 pieces, of which nearly all were subsequently melted. The late author of the sovereign reference, Michael A. Marsh, rates this issue R2 or "very rare." In the present Gem condition of this astounding piece, of course, it is much rarer still. This is an absolutely pristine Gem with golden toning and superb definition, the only certified MS65 example of the issue at PCGS, and there are none finer (8/09). The Belzberg example was an MS63.
*From the Canadiana Collection*
Estimate: $15,000-$20,000  Starting Bid: $7,500

**20353  George V gold Sovereign 1911-C,** KM20, MS67 PCGS, bust left/St. George slaying the dragon, date in exergue below, Ex: Campbell. The 1911-C production, first of the George V issues, was relatively generous at 256,946 pieces. compared to the preceding two years' productions for the 1909-C and 1910-C of 16,273 and 28,012 pieces, respectively. This is a relatively large production for the Ottawa Mint, although sovereign collectors should note that it is still a fraction of most of the Edward VII multimillion-coin mintages of Melbourne, Perth, or Sydney. Furthermore, perhaps 99% of the sovereigns of any issue from the 1920s/1930s and before have long since been melted. Nonetheless, a larger production increases the chances for the occasional phenomenal Gem coin, or even Premium Gem and Superb Gem examples. *The present MS67 is one of the two finest certified at PCGS, not only of the 1911-C issue, but among all Canadian sovereigns.*

The surfaces are a lovely, consistent apricot-gold, and even a strong loupe fails to locate any mentionable distractions. For pedigree purposes we note a tiny spot of copper toning in the reverse field, and a small curving mark in the right field, possibly as produced. The obverse is essentially pristine, and to mention any tiny marks would be to overemphasize them. The full strike has boldly articulated the King's beard, along with all of the fine details on the brilliant Pistrucci reverse. Suffice it to say that this is one of the finest circulation strike sovereigns that any collector can ever hope to see.
*From the Canadiana Collection*
Estimate: $15,000-$20,000  Starting Bid: $7,500

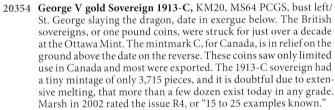

**20354** **George V gold Sovereign 1913-C,** KM20, MS64 PCGS, bust left/ St. George slaying the dragon, date in exergue below. The British sovereigns, or one pound coins, were struck for just over a decade at the Ottawa Mint. The mintmark C, for Canada, is in relief on the ground above the date on the reverse. These coins saw only limited use in Canada and most were exported. The 1913-C sovereign had a tiny mintage of only 3,715 pieces, and it is doubtful due to extensive melting, that more than a few dozen exist today in any grade. Marsh in 2002 rated the issue R4, or "15 to 25 examples known."

Attractive orange-gold patina covers both sides, with occasional hints of lilac in the fields. A few minuscule abrasions limit the grade, but none are of any significance. Flashy luster highlights the boldly struck design elements. An appealing representative. PCGS Population: 20 in 64, 0 finer (7/09).
*From the Canadiana Collection*
Estimate: $4,000-$6,000  Starting Bid: $2,000

**20355** **George V gold Sovereign 1914-C,** KM20, MS66 PCGS, bust left/ St. George slaying the dragon, date in exergue below. An astonishing Premium Gem of this low-mintage (and high-meltage) issue. The original production was only 14,891 pieces, and Michael A. Marsh in *The Gold Sovereign* reference apparently assumed a meltage of 99% for most of these early issues. So it should come as little surprise that this MS66 coin is tied for finest certified of the issue at PCGS (8/09); what is more surprising is that there are two pieces graded so fine (or one twice, always a possibility). Marsh assigns the 1914-C an R3 rarity rating, or "extremely rare." Medium golden-orange patina with full luster and a sharp strike.
*From the Canadiana Collection*
Estimate: $8,000-$10,000  Starting Bid: $4,000

## Fantastic MS65 1916-C Sovereign

**20356** **George V gold Sovereign 1916-C,** KM20, MS65 PCGS, bust left/St. George slaying the dragon, date in exergue below. Among Canadian sovereigns, while the Specimen-only 1908-C and regular-issue 1913-C have smaller mintages than the 1916-C, the 1916-C is assuredly the most valuable. Only a tiny fraction of the 6,111 pieces in the stated mintage have ever turned up, and the vast majority must be considered lost. The following appears in *Charlton's Catalogue:*

"The 1916-C issue is rare, with about fifty or so pieces known. Most of the small mintage may have been melted, accounting for the rarity, although this is by no means an established fact. ... Another tale told about the 1916-C sovereign is that the mintage was lost at sea on its way to England during World War I, as part of an international settlement. This is not established fact, only rumor."

The passage goes on to note dryly, "If there was to be a gold exchange between Canada and England in 1916, the gold needed only to be deposited with the New York Federal Reserve for the account of Great Britain, and not subjected to a perilous sea voyage during a time of war."

This elegant example has a rich, original "skin" on it, with ample patina over warm butter-yellow surfaces. The luster is soft but pleasing, and the strike is above-average. Most remarkable about this coin is its surface quality; there are no individually mentionable abrasions, and the best pedigree marker is a tiny dot of alloy just to the right of the horse's head. A wonderful Gem, tied with just one other example for finest certified by PCGS (7/09).
*From the Canadiana Collection*
Estimate: $125,000-$175,000 Starting Bid: $62,500

**20357** **George V gold Sovereign 1917-C,** KM20, MS64 PCGS, bust left/ St. George slaying the dragon, date in exergue below, Ex: Pittman. Although not as common as the 1911-C, the 1917-C sovereign is a plentiful issue in most grades. PCGS, however, has certified no examples finer than the present coin (7/09). Wafts of light green accent the mostly orange-gold patina that envelops the lustrous surfaces. The surfaces are remarkably clean, and the strike is crisp. Pittman bought this attractive piece for only $35 in the 1950s.
*From the Canadiana Collection*
Estimate: $1,000-$1,200  Starting Bid: $500

**20358** **George V gold Sovereign 1918-C,** KM20, MS64 PCGS, bust left/ St. George slaying the dragon, date in exergue below. The 1918-C sovereign is rare at this lofty level, and PCGS has certified just two MS64 examples, with none finer (7/09). Charming yellow-gold patina drapes both sides of this lightly abraded near-Gem. The King's hair is a touch soft, but the details are otherwise sharply defined. Coruscating satiny luster enhances the eye appeal. An excellent example for the specialist.
*From the Canadiana Collection*
Estimate: $1,500-$2,000  Starting Bid: $750

**20359** **George V gold Sovereign 1919-C,** KM20, MS64 PCGS, bust left/ St. George slaying the dragon, date in exergue below. This was the last year that sovereigns were struck in Canada, an issue that Michael A. Marsh rates as "scarce." Captivating luster radiates from the lovely apricot-gold surfaces. Several minor abrasions preclude a Gem designation. Numerous die polish lines are seen in the fields. This well-struck Choice Uncirculated example has great eye appeal. PCGS has certified a couple of dozen coins in MS64, all tied for finest (8/09).
*From the Canadiana Collection*
Estimate: $1,500-$2,000  Starting Bid: $750

**20360** **George V gold Five Dollars 1912,** KM26, MS65 PCGS, Ex: Campbell. When the Ottawa Mint opened in 1908 (the first coins were struck on January 2), it was planned that both 1 Pound and decimal gold coins would be struck. A small number of Specimen-format sovereigns (1 Pound coins) were issued in 1908, and regular production began the following year. The preparations for decimal gold coins (5 and 10 Dollar pieces) were slower, and the final designs went unfinished until 1911. The first examples were struck in 1912, and unlike the sovereigns they bore no C mintmark.

Delightful yellow-gold patina embraces the carefully preserved surfaces. There are only a few wispy luster grazes on the obverse, while the reverse is nearly perfect. The strike is razor-sharp. Scintillating satiny enhances the eye appeal. PCGS Population: 11 in 65, 2 finer (7/09).
*From the Canadiana Collection*
Estimate: $3,000-$5,000  Starting Bid: $1,500

**20361 George V gold Five Dollars 1913,** KM26, MS64 PCGS. The 1913 has a lower mintage than the 1912 5 Dollar piece and is scarcer in high grades. Dazzling cartwheel luster radiates beneath the lovely pale yellow patina. Several minuscule handling marks keep this piece from an even higher grade. The strike is bold, and the eye appeal is excellent. PCGS has certified no examples finer (7/09). *From the Canadiana Collection*
Estimate: $1,000-$1,200  Starting Bid: $500

To view all the Worlds Coins we have to offer in this Auction please see our seperate catalogs or go online to HA.com/WorldCoins

**20362 George V gold Five Dollars 1914,** KM26, MS64 PCGS. Wartime demands prompted legislation that restricted the flow of gold and brought an end to the 5 and 10 Dollar pieces. Additionally, Canadian paper money could no longer be redeemed for gold coins. The 1914 5 Dollars, the final issue in the short-lived series, had a low mintage of just 31,122 pieces and is significantly more challenging than the 1912 and 1913. PCGS has certified only four examples in MS64, with none finer (7/09).

Hints of rose-red in the margins enhance the mostly light yellow patina that drapes both sides. The design elements are sharply struck, and there are no significant marks. Splendid luster fills the fields. An appealing example of this scarce issue. *From the Canadiana Collection*
Estimate: $5,000-$7,000  Starting Bid: $2,500

# Gold 10 Dollars 1912—Finest Certified of the Type and Issue

**20363  George V gold 10 Dollars 1912,** KM27, MS66 PCGS, Ex: Campbell. A glorious reddish-gold Premium Gem example of this scarce first-year gold issue, produced to the extent of only 74,759 coins. In MS66, this is one of only two such coins so certified at PCGS, and there are *none finer for either the issue or the type,* since PCGS has never certified a 1913 or 1914 10 Dollar higher than MS65. (Indeed, there are precious few MS65 examples surviving.) Full mint bloom is widely evident on both sides of this splendid reddish-orange coin. The strike is boldly impressed throughout, and the few trivial ticks seen in the obverse fields are not at all distracting. An unimprovable coin and a significant opportunity to acquire one of the finest Canadian gold coins available.

The Ottawa Mint was established in 1908 as a branch of the Royal Mint, and from its inception it was planned that gold coins should be issued in four different decimal dollar denominations from 2.5 Dollars to 20 Dollars, along with British sovereigns (1 Pound coins). Plans proceeded slowly, however: While sovereigns were produced beginning in 1908 bearing the C mintmark, the first dollar-denominated gold was produced only four years later, in 1912, by which time the 2.5 and 20 Dollar denominations had been dropped from the production schedule. There was no mintmark.

The George V 10 Dollar gold was produced only from 1912 to 1914, at which time changes in wartime legislation restricted the flow of gold and Dominion banks stopped currency redemptions in the precious metal. George V had become King and Emperor of India only two years before this coin was produced, in 1910 when his father, Edward VII, died.
*From the Canadiana Collection*
Estimate: $25,000-$35,000  Starting Bid: $12,500

**20364  George V gold 10 Dollars 1913,** KM27, MS64 PCGS. Despite having a mintage about twice that of the previous year, the 1913 is more elusive in Mint State. According to the PCGS population data, it is also scarcer than the 1914, which had a similar mintage. PCGS has certified only five examples, and none are finer (7/09). This resplendent near-Gem has a delightful rosy hue in the fields and attractive yellow-gold patina elsewhere. Dazzling satiny luster radiates from the obverse, while the reverse has eye-catching semi-prooflike reflectivity. A few minuscule abrasions do not distract. The strike is nearly full.
*From the Canadiana Collection*
Estimate: $7,500-$10,000   Starting Bid: $3,750

## Gold 10 Dollars 1914 MS65—Sole Finest Certified at PCGS

20365  **George V gold 10 Dollars 1914,** KM27, MS65 PCGS, the key to the George V type in high grade, despite the production of 140,068 coins—only a bit less than the 1913, and nearly twice as much as the first-year 1912. This is the *single finest graded and only Gem of the issue so certified at PCGS (7/09),* a remarkable coin and an unparalleled opportunity for dedicated collectors of Canadian coins. In our January 2003 catalog of the Sid and Alicia Belzberg Collection of Canadian Coinage, we wrote of an MS63 PCGS example, "It was long thought that this issue was the unquestioned key date of the type. In recent years, general thinking is that more examples of this date are available in MS63 than the 1913, but the number in MS64 is approximately the same."

Of course this example, the sole MS65 certified by PCGS of the issue, was a coin not even remotely contemplated in the above quote. This piece boasts lovely reddish-bronze patina over problem-free surfaces with a generous quotient of eye appeal. Minuscule contact marks in the fields, primarily the obverse, along with a single tick on the monarch's beard, appear to account for the grade assigned. As there are no MS65 examples of the 1913 certified at PCGS and this piece is the only Gem 1914, the present example must be considered among the most desirable of the entire George V 10 Dollar type.
*From the Canadiana Collection*
Estimate: $30,000-$40,000  Starting Bid: $15,000

*End of the Canadiana Collection*

# Heritage Auction Galleries Staff

### Steve Ivy - Co-Chairman and CEO

Steve Ivy began collecting and studying rare coins as a youth, and as a teenager began advertising coins for sale in national publications in 1963. Seven years later, at the age of 20, he opened for business in downtown Dallas, and in 1976, incorporated as an auction company. Steve managed the business as well as serving as chief buyer, buying and selling hundreds of millions of dollars of coins during the 1970s and early 1980s. In early 1983, James Halperin became a full partner, and the name of the corporation was changed to Heritage Auctions. Steve's primary responsibilities now include management of the marketing and selling efforts of the company, the formation of corporate policy for long-term growth, and corporate relations with financial institutions. He remains intimately involved in all the various categories Heritage Auctions deals in today. Steve engages in daily discourse with industry leaders on all aspects of the fine art and collectibles business, and his views on market trends and developments are respected throughout the industry. He previously served on both the Board of Directors of the Professional Numismatists Guild (past president), and The Industry Council for Tangible Assets (past Chairman). Steve's keen appreciation of history is reflected in his active participation in other organizations, including past board positions on the Texas Historical Foundation and the Dallas Historical Society (where he also served as Exhibits Chairman). Steve is an avid collector of Texas books, manuscripts, and national currency, and he owns one of the largest and finest collections in private hands. He is also a past Board Chair of Dallas Challenge, and is currently the Finance Chair of the Phoenix House of Texas.

### James Halperin - Co-Chairman

Born in Boston in 1952, Jim formed a part-time rare coin business at age 15 after discovering he had a knack (along with a nearly photographic memory) for coins. Jim scored a perfect 800 on his math SATs and received early acceptance to Harvard College, but after attending three semesters took a permanent leave of absence to pursue his full-time numismatic career. In 1975, Jim supervised the protocols for the first mainframe computer system in the numismatic business, which would catapult New England Rare Coin Galleries to the top of the industry in less than four years. In 1982, Jim's business merged with that of his friend and former archrival Steve Ivy. Their partnership has become Heritage Auctions, the third-largest auction house in the world. Jim is also a well-known futurist, an active collector of EC comics and early 20th-century American art (visit www.jhalpe.com), venture capital investor, philanthropist (he endows a multimillion-dollar health education foundation), and part-time novelist. His first fiction book, *The Truth Machine*, was published in 1996, became an international science fiction bestseller, and was optioned for movie development by Warner Brothers and Lions Gate. Jim's second novel, *The First Immortal*, was published in early 1998 and immediately optioned as a Hallmark Hall of Fame television miniseries.

### Greg Rohan - President

At the age of eight, Greg Rohan started collecting coins as well as buying them for resale to his schoolmates. By 1971, at the age of 10, he was already buying and selling coins from a dealer's table at trade shows in his hometown of Seattle. His business grew rapidly, and by 1985 he had offices in both Seattle and Minneapolis. He joined Heritage in 1987 as Executive Vice-President. Today, as a partner and as President of Heritage, his responsibilities include overseeing the firm's private client group and working with top collectors in every field in which Heritage is active. Greg has been involved with many of the rarest items and most important collections handled by the firm, including the purchase and/or sale of the Ed Trompeter Collection (the world's largest numismatic purchase according to the Guinness Book of World Records). During his career, Greg has handled more than $1 billion of rare coins, collectibles and art. He has provided expert testimony for the United States Attorneys in San Francisco, Dallas, and Philadelphia, and for the Federal Trade Commission (FTC). He has worked with collectors, consignors, and their advisors regarding significant collections of books, manuscripts, comics, currency, jewelry, vintage movie posters, sports and entertainment memorabilia, decorative arts, and fine art. Greg is a past Chapter Chairman for North Texas of the Young Presidents' Organization (YPO), and is an active supporter of the arts. Greg co-authored "The Collectors Estate Handbook," winner of the NLG's Robert Friedberg Award for numismatic book of the year. He previously served on the seven-person Advisory Board to the Federal Reserve Bank of Dallas, in his second appointed term.

### Paul Minshull - Chief Operating Officer

As Chief Operating Officer, Paul Minshull's managerial responsibilities include integrating sales, personnel, inventory, security and MIS for Heritage. His major accomplishments include overseeing the hardware migration from mainframe to PC, the software migration of all inventory and sales systems, and implementation of a major Internet presence. Heritage's successful employee-suggestion program has generated 200 or more ideas each month since 1995, and has helped increase employee productivity, expand business, and improve employee retention. Paul oversees the company's highly-regarded IT department, and has been the driving force behind Heritage's Web development, now a significant portion of Heritage's future plans. As the first auction house that combined traditional floor bidding with active Internet bidding, the totally interactive system has catapulted Heritage to the top collectible and Fine Art website (Forbes Magazine's "Best of the Web"). Paul came to Heritage in 1984. Since 1987, he has been Chief Operating Officer for all Heritage companies and affiliates.

### Todd Imhof - Executive Vice President

Unlike most of his contemporaries, Todd Imhof did not start collecting in his teens. Shortly after graduating college, Todd declined offers from prestigious Wall Street banks to join a former classmate at a small rare coin firm in the Seattle area. In the mid-1980s, the rare coin industry was rapidly changing, with the advent of third-party grading and growing computer technologies. As a newcomer, Todd more easily embraced these new dynamics and quickly emerged as a highly respected dealer. In 1991, he co-founded Pinnacle Rarities, a firm specialized in servicing the savviest and most preeminent collectors in numismatics. At only 25, he was accepted into the PNG, and currently serves on its Consumer Protection Committee and its Legislation/Taxation Issues Committee. In 1992, he was invited to join the Board of Directors for the Industry Council for Tangible Assets, later serving as its Chairman (2002-2005). Since joining Heritage in 2006, Todd continues to advise most of Heritage's largest and most prominent clients.

**Leo Frese - Vice President**
Leo has been involved in numismatics for nearly 40 years, a professional numismatist since 1971, and has been with Heritage for more than 20 years. He literally worked his way up the Heritage "ladder," working with Bob Merrill for nearly 15 years, then becoming Director of Consignments. Leo has been actively involved in assisting clients sell nearly $500,000,000 in numismatic material. Leo was recently accepted as a member of PNG, is a life member of the ANA, and holds membership in FUN, CSNS, and other numismatic organizations.

**Jim Stoutjesdyk - Vice President**
Jim Stoutjesdyk was named Vice President of Heritage Rare Coin Galleries in 2004. He was named ANA's Outstanding Young Numismatist of the Year in 1987. A University of Michigan graduate, he was first employed by Superior Galleries, eventually becoming their Director of Collector Sales. Since joining Heritage in 1993, Jim has served in many capacities. Jim's duties now include buying and selling, pricing all new purchases, assisting with auction estimates and reserves, and overseeing the daily operations of the rare coin department.

**Norma L. Gonzalez - VP of Auction Operations**
Norma Gonzalez joined the U.S. Navy in August of 1993 and received her Bachelor's Degree in Resource Management. She joined Heritage in 1998 and was promoted to Vice President in 2003. She currently manages the operations departments, including Coins, Currency, World & Ancient Coins, Sportscards & Memorabilia, Comics, Movie Posters, Pop Culture and Political Memorabilia.

**Debbie Rexing - VP - Marketing**
Debbie Rexing joined the Heritage team in 2001 and her marketing credentials include degrees in Business Administration and Human Resources from The Ohio State University. Debbie has worked across many categories within the company leading to her comprehensive and integrative approach to the job. She guides all aspects of Heritage's print marketing strategies – advertisements, brochures, direct mail campaigns, coordination of print buying, catalog design and production, The Heritage Magazine, and media and press relations.

**Ron Brackemyre - Vice President**
Ron Brackemyre began his career at Heritage Auction Galleries in 1998 as the Manager of the Shipping Department, was promoted to Consignment Operations Manager for Numismatics in 2004 and in 2009 added oversight of the entire photography operation at Heritage, wherein his department coordinates all photography, scanning and photoshopping. He is also responsible for the security of all of Heritage's coin and currency consignments, both at the Dallas world headquarters and at shows, as well as cataloging of coins for upcoming auctions, coordination of auction planning, security and transportation logistics, lot-view, auction prep and oversight for the entire shipping department.

**Marti Korver - Manager - Credit/Collections**
Marti Korver was recruited out of the banking profession by Jim Ruddy, and she worked with Paul Rynearson, Karl Stephens, and Judy Cahn on ancients and world coins at Bowers & Ruddy Galleries, in Hollywood, CA. She migrated into the coin auction business, and represented bidders as agent at B&R auctions for 10 years. She also worked as a research assistant for Q. David Bowers for several years.

**Mark Prendergast - Director, Trusts & Estates**
Mark Prendergast earned his degree in Art History from Vanderbilt University and began his career in the arts working with a national dealer in private sales of 20th Century American Art. Joining Christie's in 1998 and advancing during a 10 year tenure to the position of Vice President, he was instrumental in bringing to market many important and prominent works of art, collections and estates. Having established a Houston office for Heritage, he serves as Director of Business Development, Trusts & Estates, providing assistance to fiduciary professionals and private clients with appraisals, collection assessments and auction consignments in all areas of art and collectibles.

# World Coin Department

**Warren Tucker- Director of World Coin Auctions**
Warren Tucker has been a full-time coin dealer since 1964. In 1968, he joined Jack Boozer and Doug Weaver in business in Waco, Texas, where he first met Steve Ivy. Warren later moved back to Georgia, where he became a partner with John Hamrick at WorldWide Coin Investments of Atlanta. During the 1970s, Warren began more extensive travel throughout Europe and Asia to buy coins. In 1979, he first joined forces with Steve Ivy, opening an office in Atlanta. Associations with Richard Nelson and Ronald J. Gillio followed thereafter.

**Cristiano Bierrenbach - Director of International Sales**
Cristiano Bierrenbach received a degree in management from Bucknell University in Pennsylvania in 1996. In 1999, Cristiano founded Bier Numismatica and within a few years had become one of the largest numismatic dealers in Latin America. At the age of 30, he became the youngest ever Technical Director of the Brazilian Numismatic Society, and is the founder of the Latin American Numismatic Convention. He is a life member of the ANA and FUN and several other numismatic clubs and organizations around the world.

**Scott Cordry - Assistant Director of World Coin Auctions**
Scott Cordry graduated from UC Berkeley with "great distinction" and Phi Beta Kappa honors. After college, he worked for Worldwide Coins in Atlanta for a few months before going into business for himself, and then in partnership with Freeman Craig. In 1975, Scott again decided to pursue world coins independently, and he has been in the foreign coin business ever since. Scott is a member of the ANA, NI, AINA, ONS and IBNS, and has been a member of the IAPN as well, from 1979-1993. Scott has been cataloging world coins for Heritage World Coin Auctions since October of 2002.

**Cataloged by:** Jon Amato, John Beety, Cris Bierrenbach, Mark Borckardt, Scott Cordry, George Huber, John Lavender, Bruce Lorich, Stuart Rubenfeld, Max Spiegel, Warren Tucker, Mark VanWinkle

**Edited by:** Scott Cordry, Danita Glenn, Warren Tucker

**Operations Support by:** Erika Cantu, Danita Glenn, Cristina Gonzalez, Manuela Beuno, Maria Flores, SanJuana Gonzales, Cristina Ibarra, Cinthya Pina, Jose Martinez

**Catalog and Internet Imaging by:** Travis Awalt, Maribel Cazares, Joel Gonzalez, Sharon Johnson, Darnell McCown, Colleen McInerney, Nancy Ramos, Tony Webb, Jason Young

**Production and Design by:** Matt Pegues, Mark Masat, Mary Hermann, Debbie Rexing

# Terms and Conditions of Auction

**Auctioneer and Auction:**

1. This Auction is presented by Heritage Auction Galleries, a d/b/a/ of Heritage Auctions, Inc., or its affiliates Heritage Numismatic Auctions, Inc., or Heritage Vintage Sports Auctions, Inc., or Currency Auctions of America, Inc., as identified with the applicable licensing information on the title page of the catalog or on the HA.com Internet site (the "Auctioneer"). The Auction is conducted under these Terms and Conditions of Auction and applicable state and local law. Announcements and corrections from the podium and those made through the Terms and Conditions of Auctions appearing on the Internet at HA.com supersede those in the printed catalog.

**Buyer's Premium:**

2. On bids placed through Auctioneer, a Buyer's Premium of fifteen percent (15%) will be added to the successful hammer price bid on lots in Coin, Currency, and Philatelic auctions or nineteen and one-half percent (19.5%) on lots in all other auctions. There is a minimum Buyer's Premium of $14.00 per lot. In Gallery Auctions (sealed bid auctions of mostly bulk numismatic material), the Buyer's Premium is 19.5%.

**Auction Venues:**

3. The following Auctions are conducted solely on the Internet: Heritage Weekly Internet Auctions (Coin, Currency, Comics, and Vintage Movie Poster); Heritage Monthly Internet Auctions (Sports, and Stamps). Signature® Auctions and Grand Format Auctions accept bids from the Internet, telephone, fax, or mail first, followed by a floor bidding session; Heritage Live and real-time telephone bidding are available to registered clients during these auctions.

**Bidders:**

4. Any person participating or registering for the Auction agrees to be bound by and accepts these Terms and Conditions of Auction ("Bidder(s)").
5. All Bidders must meet Auctioneer's qualifications to bid. Any Bidder who is not a client in good standing of the Auctioneer may be disqualified at Auctioneer's sole option and will not be awarded lots. Such determination may be made by Auctioneer in its sole and unlimited discretion, at any time prior to, during, or even after the close of the Auction. Auctioneer reserves the right to exclude any person from the auction.
6. If an entity places a bid, then the person executing the bid on behalf of the entity agrees to personally guarantee payment for any successful bid.

**Credit:**

7. Bidders who have not established credit with the Auctioneer must either furnish satisfactory credit information (including two collectibles-related business references) well in advance of the Auction or supply valid credit card information. Bids placed through our Interactive Internet program will only be accepted from pre-registered Bidders; Bidders who are not members of HA.com or affiliates should pre-register at least 48 hours before the start of the first session (exclusive of holidays or weekends) to allow adequate time to contact references. Credit may be granted at the discretion of Auctioneer. Additionally Bidders who have not previously established credit or who wish to bid in excess of their established credit history may be required to provide their social security number or the last four digits thereof to us so a credit check may be performed prior to Auctioneer's acceptance of a bid.

**Bidding Options:**

8. Bids in Signature® Auctions or Grand Format Auctions may be placed as set forth in the printed catalog section entitled "Choose your bidding method." For auctions held solely on the Internet, see the alternatives on HA.com. Review at HA.com/common/howtobid.php.
9. Presentment of Bids: Non-Internet bids (including but not limited to podium, fax, phone and mail bids) are treated similar to floor bids in that they must be on-increment or at a half increment (called a cut bid). Any podium, fax, phone, or mail bids that do not conform to a full or half increment will be rounded up or down to the nearest full or half increment and this revised amount will be considered your high bid.
10. Auctioneer's Execution of Certain Bids. Auctioneer cannot be responsible for your errors in bidding, so carefully check that every bid is entered correctly. When identical mail or FAX bids are submitted, preference is given to the first received. To ensure the greatest accuracy, your written bids should be entered on the standard printed bid sheet and be received at Auctioneer's place of business at least two business days before the Auction start. Auctioneer is not responsible for executing mail bids or FAX bids received on or after the day the first lot is sold, nor Internet bids submitted after the published closing time; nor is Auctioneer responsible for proper execution of bids submitted by telephone, mail, FAX, e-mail, Internet, or in person once the Auction begins. Internet bids may not be withdrawn until your written request is received and acknowledged by Auctioneer (FAX: 214-4438425); such requests must state the reason, and may constitute grounds for withdrawal of bidding privileges. Lots won by mail Bidders will not be delivered at the Auction unless prearranged.
11. Caveat as to Bid Increments. Bid increments (over the current bid level) determine the lowest amount you may bid on a particular lot. Bids greater than one increment over the current bid can be any whole dollar amount. It is possible under several circumstances for winning bids to be between increments, sometimes only $1 above the previous increment. Please see: "How can I lose by less than an increment?" on our website. Bids will be accepted in whole dollar amounts only. No "buy" or "unlimited" bids will be accepted.

The following chart governs current bidding increments.

| Current Bid | Bid Increment | Current Bid | Bid Increment |
|---|---|---|---|
| <$10 | $1 | $20,000 - $29,999 | $2,000 |
| $10 - $29 | $2 | $30,000 - $49,999 | $2,500 |
| $30 - $49 | $3 | $50,000 - $99,999 | $5,000 |
| $50 - $99 | $5 | $100,000 - $199,999 | $10,000 |
| $100 - $199 | $10 | $200,000 - $299,999 | $20,000 |
| $200 - $299 | $20 | $300,000 - $499,999 | $25,000 |
| $300 - $499 | $25 | $500,000 - $999,999 | $50,000 |
| $500 - $999 | $50 | $1,000,000 - $1,999,999 | $100,000 |
| $1,000 - $1,999 | $100 | $2,000,000 - $2,999,999 | $200,000 |
| $2,000 - $2,999 | $200 | $3,000,000 - $4,999,999 | $250,000 |
| $3,000 - $4,999 | $250 | $5,000,000 - $9,999,999 | $500,000 |
| $5,000 - $9,999 | $500 | >$10,000,000 | $1,000,000 |
| $10,000 - $19,999 | $1,000 | | |

12. If Auctioneer calls for a full increment, a bidder may request Auctioneer to accept a bid at half of the increment ("Cut Bid") only once per lot. After offering a Cut Bid, bidders may continue to participate only at full increments. Off-increment bids may be accepted by the Auctioneer at Signature® Auctions and Grand Format Auctions. If the Auctioneer solicits bids other than the expected increment, these bids will not be considered Cut Bids.

**Conducting the Auction:**

13. Notice of the consignor's liberty to place bids on his lots in the Auction is hereby made in accordance with Article 2 of the Texas Business and Commercial Code. A "Minimum Bid" is an amount below which the lot will not sell. THE CONSIGNOR OF PROPERTY MAY PLACE WRITTEN "Minimum Bids" ON HIS LOTS IN ADVANCE OF THE AUCTION; ON SUCH LOTS, IF THE HAMMER PRICE DOES NOT MEET THE "Minimum Bid", THE CONSIGNOR MAY PAY A REDUCED COMMISSION ON THOSE LOTS. "Minimum Bids" are generally posted online several days prior to the Auction closing. For any successful bid placed by a consignor on his Property on the Auction floor, or by any means during the live session, or after the "Minimum Bid" for an Auction have been posted, we will require the consignor to pay full Buyer's Premium and Seller's Commissions on such lot.
14. The highest qualified Bidder recognized by the Auctioneer shall be the buyer. In the event of any dispute between any Bidders at an Auction, Auctioneer may at his sole discretion reoffer the lot. Auctioneer's decision and declaration of the winning Bidder shall be final and binding upon all Bidders. Bids properly offered, whether by floor Bidder or other means of bidding, may on occasion be missed or go unrecognized; in such cases, the Auctioneer may declare the recognized bid accepted as the winning bid, regardless of whether a competing bid may have been higher.
15. Auctioneer reserves the right to refuse to honor any bid or to limit the amount of any bid, in its sole discretion. A bid is considered not made in "Good Faith" when made by an insolvent or irresponsible person, a person under the age of eighteen, or is not supported by satisfactory credit, collectibles references, or otherwise. Regardless of the disclosure of his identity, any bid by a consignor or his agent on a lot consigned by him is deemed to be made in "Good Faith." Any person apparently appearing on the OFAC list is not eligible to bid.
16. Nominal Bids. The Auctioneer in its sole discretion may reject nominal bids, small opening bids, or very nominal advances. If a lot bearing estimates fails to open for 40–60% of the low estimate, the Auctioneer may pass the item or may place a protective bid on behalf of the consignor.
17. Lots bearing bidding estimates shall open at Auctioneer's discretion (approximately 50%-60% of the low estimate). In the event that no bid meets or exceeds that opening amount, the lot shall pass as unsold.
18. All items are to be purchased per lot as numerically indicated and no lots will be broken. Auctioneer reserves the right to withdraw, prior to the close, any lots from the Auction.
19. Auctioneer reserves the right to rescind the sale in the event of nonpayment, breach of a warranty, disputed ownership, auctioneer's clerical error or omission in exercising bids and reserves, or for any other reason and in Auctioneer's sole discretion. In cases of nonpayment, Auctioneer's election to void a sale does not relieve the Bidder from their obligation to pay Auctioneer its fees (seller's and buyer's premium) and any other damages or expenses pertaining to the lot.
20. Auctioneer occasionally experiences Internet and/or Server service outages, and Auctioneer periodically schedules system downtime for maintenance and other purposes, during which Bidders cannot participate or place bids. If such outages occur, we may at our discretion extend bidding for the Auction. Bidders unable to place their Bids through the Internet are directed to contact Client Services at 1-800-872-6467.
21. The Auctioneer or its affiliates may consign items to be sold in the Auction, and may bid on those lots or any other lots. Auctioneer or affiliates expressly reserve the right to modify any such bids at any time prior to the hammer based upon data made known to the Auctioneer or its affiliates. The Auctioneer may extend advances, guarantees, or loans to certain consignors, and may extend financing or other credits at varying rates to certain Bidders in the auction.
22. The Auctioneer has the right to sell certain unsold items after the close of the Auction. Such lots shall be considered sold during the Auction and all these Terms and Conditions shall apply to such sales including but not limited to the Buyer's Premium, return rights, and disclaimers.

**Payment:**

23. All sales are strictly for cash in United States dollars (including U.S. currency, bank wire, cashier checks, travelers checks, eChecks, and bank money orders, all subject to reporting requirements). All are subject to clearing and funds being received In Auctioneer's account before delivery of the purchases. Auctioneer reserves the right to determine if a check constitutes "good funds" when drawn on a U.S. bank for ten days, and thirty days when drawn on an international bank. Credit Card (Visa or Master Card only) and PayPal payments may be accepted up to $10,000 from non-dealers at the sole discretion of the Auctioneer, subject to the following limitations: a) sales are only to the cardholder, b) purchases are shipped to the cardholder's registered and verified address, c) Auctioneer may pre-approve the cardholder's credit line, d) a credit card transaction may not be used in conjunction with any other financing or extended terms offered by the Auctioneer, and must transact immediately upon invoice presentation, e) rights of return are governed by these Terms and Conditions, which supersede those conditions promulgated by the card issuer, f) floor Bidders must present their card.
24. Payment is due upon closing of the Auction session, or upon presentment of an invoice. Auctioneer reserves the right to void an invoice if payment in full is not received within 7 days after the close of the Auction. In cases of nonpayment, Auctioneer's election to void a sale does not relieve the Bidder from their obligation to pay Auctioneer its fees (seller's and buyer's premium) on the lot and any other damages pertaining to the lot.
25. Lots delivered to you, or your representative in the States of Texas, California, **New York**, or other states where the Auction may be held, are subject to all applicable state and local taxes, unless appropriate permits are on file with Auctioneer. Bidder agrees to pay Auctioneer the actual amount of tax due in the event that sales tax is not properly collected due to: 1) an expired, inaccurate, inappropriate tax certificate or declaration, 2) an incorrect interpretation of the applicable statute, 3) or any other reason. The appropriate form or certificate must be on file at and verified by Auctioneer five days prior to Auction or tax must be paid; only if such form or certificate is received by Auctioneer within 4 days after the Auction can a refund of tax paid be made. Lots from different Auctions may not be aggregated for sales tax purposes.
26. In the event that a Bidder's payment is dishonored upon presentment(s), Bidder shall pay the maximum statutory processing fee set by applicable state law. If you attempt to pay via eCheck and your financial institution denies this transfer from your bank account, or the payment cannot be completed using the selected funding source, you agree to complete payment using your credit card on file.
27. If any Auction invoice submitted by Auctioneer is not paid in full when due, the unpaid balance will bear interest at the highest rate permitted by law from the date of invoice until paid. Any invoice not paid when due will bear a three percent (3%) late fee on the invoice amount or three percent (3%) of any installment that is past due. If the Auctioneer refers any invoice to an attorney for collection, the buyer agrees to pay attorney's fees, court costs, and other collection costs incurred by Auctioneer. If Auctioneer assigns collection to its in-house legal staff, such attorney's time expended on the matter shall be compensated at a rate comparable to the hourly rate of independent attorneys.
28. In the event a successful Bidder fails to pay any amounts due, Auctioneer reserves the right to sell the lot(s) securing the invoice to any underbidders in the Auction that the lot(s) appeared, or at subsequent private or public sale, or relist the lot(s) in a future auction conducted by Auctioneer. A defaulting Bidder agrees to pay for the reasonable costs of resale (including a 10% seller's commission, if consigned to an auction conducted by Auctioneer). The defaulting Bidder is liable to pay any difference between his total original invoice for the lot(s), plus any applicable interest, and the net proceeds for the lot(s) if sold at private sale or the subsequent hammer price of the lot(s) less the 10% seller's commissions, if sold at an Auctioneer's auction.

29. Auctioneer reserves the right to require payment in full in good funds before delivery of the merchandise.
30. Auctioneer shall have a lien against the merchandise purchased by the buyer to secure payment of the Auction invoice. Auctioneer is further granted a lien and the right to retain possession of any other property of the buyer then held by the Auctioneer or its affiliates to secure payment of any Auction invoice or any other amounts due the Auctioneer or affiliates from the buyer. With respect to these lien rights, Auctioneer shall have all the rights of a secured creditor under Article 9 of the Texas Uniform Commercial Code, including but not limited to the right of sale. In addition, with respect to payment of the Auction invoice(s), the buyer waives any and all rights of offset he might otherwise have against the Auctioneer and the consignor of the merchandise included on the invoice. If a Bidder owes Auctioneer or its affiliates on any account, Auctioneer and its affiliates shall have the right to offset such unpaid account by any credit balance due Bidder, and it may secure by possessory lien any unpaid amount by any of the Bidder's property in their possession.
31. Title shall not pass to the successful Bidder until all invoices are paid in full. It is the responsibility of the buyer to provide adequate insurance coverage for the items once they have been delivered to a common carrier or third-party shipper.

**Delivery; Shipping; and Handling Charges:**

32. Buyer is liable for shipping and handling. Please refer to Auctioneer's website www.HA.com/common/shipping.php for the latest charges or call Auctioneer. Auctioneer is unable to combine purchases from other auctions or affiliates into one package for shipping purposes. Lots won will be shipped in a commercially reasonable time after payment in good funds for the merchandise and the shipping fees is received or credit extended, except when third-party shipment occurs.
33. Successful international Bidders shall provide written shipping instructions, including specified customs declarations, to the Auctioneer for any lots to be delivered outside of the United States. NOTE: Declaration value shall be the item'(s) hammer price together with its buyer's premium and Auctioneer shall use the correct harmonized code for the lot. Domestic Buyers on lots designated for third-party shipment must designate the common carrier, accept risk of loss, and prepay shipping costs.
34. All shipping charges will be borne by the successful Bidder. Any risk of loss during shipment will be borne by the buyer following Auctioneer's delivery to the designated common carrier or third-party shipper, regardless of domestic or foreign shipment.
35. Due to the nature of some items sold, it shall be the responsibility for the successful bidder to arrange pick-up and shipping through third-parties; as to such items Auctioneer shall have no liability. Failure to pick-up or arrange shipping in a timely fashion (within ten days) shall subject Lots to storage and moving charges, including a $100 administration fee plus $10 daily storage for larger items and $5.00 daily for smaller items (storage fee per item) after 35 days. In the event the Lot is not removed within ninety days, the Lot may be offered for sale to recover any past due storage or moving fees, including a 10% Seller's Commission.
36. The laws of various countries regulate the import or export of certain plant and animal properties, including (but not limited to) items made of (or including) ivory, whalebone, turtleshell, coral, crocodile, or other wildlife. Transport of such lots may require special licenses for export, import, or both. Bidder is responsible for: 1) obtaining all information on such restricted items for both export and import; 2) obtaining all such licenses and/or permits. Delay or failure to obtain any such license or permit does not relieve the buyer of timely compliance with standard payment terms. For further information, please contact Ron Brackemyre at 800-872-6467 ext. 1312.
37. Any request for shipping verification for undelivered packages must be made within 30 days of shipment by Auctioneer.

**Cataloging, Warranties and Disclaimers:**

38. NO WARRANTY, WHETHER EXPRESSED OR IMPLIED, IS MADE WITH RESPECT TO ANY DESCRIPTION CONTAINED IN THIS AUCTION OR ANY SECOND OPINE. Any description of the items or second opine contained in this Auction is for the sole purpose of identifying the items for those Bidders who do not have the opportunity to view the lots prior to bidding, and no description of items has been made part of the basis of the bargain or has created any express warranty that the goods would conform to any description made by Auctioneer. Color variations can be expected in any electronic or printed imaging, and are not grounds for the return of any lot. NOTE: Auctioneer, in specified auction venues, for example, Fine Art, may have express written warranties and you are referred to those specific terms and conditions. .
39. Auctioneer is selling only such right or title to the items being sold as Auctioneer may have by virtue of consignment agreements on the date of auction and disclaims any warranty of title to the Property. Auctioneer disclaims any warranty of merchantability or fitness for any particular purposes. All images, descriptions, sales data, and archival records are the exclusive property of Auctioneer, and may be used by Auctioneer for advertising, promotion, archival records, and any other uses deemed appropriate.
40. Translations of foreign language documents may be provided as a convenience to interested parties. Auctioneer makes no representation as to the accuracy of those translations and will not be held responsible for errors in bidding arising from inaccuracies in translation.
41. Auctioneer disclaims all liability for damages, consequential or otherwise, arising out of or in connection with the sale of any Property by Auctioneer to Bidder. No third party may rely on any benefit of these Terms and Conditions and any rights, if any, established hereunder are personal to the Bidder and may not be assigned. Any statement made by the Auctioneer is an opinion and does not constitute a warranty or representation. No employee of Auctioneer may alter these Terms and Conditions, and, unless signed by a principal of Auctioneer, any such alteration is null and void.
42. Auctioneer shall not be liable for breakage of glass or damage to frames (patent or latent); such defects, in any event, shall not be a basis for any claim for return or reduction in purchase price.

**Release:**

43. In consideration of participation in the Auction and the placing of a bid, Bidder expressly releases Auctioneer, its officers, directors and employees, its affiliates, and its outside experts that provide second opines, from any and all claims, cause of action, chose of action, whether at law or equity or any arbitration or mediation rights existing under the rules of any professional society or affiliation based upon the assigned description, or a derivative theory, breach of warranty express or implied, representation or other matter set forth within these Terms and Conditions of Auction or otherwise. In the event of a claim, Bidder agrees that such rights and privileges conferred therein are strictly construed as specifically declared herein; e.g., authenticity, typographical error, etc. and are the exclusive remedy. Bidder, by non-compliance to these express terms of a granted remedy, shall waive any claim against Auctioneer.
44. Notice: Some Property sold by Auctioneer are inherently dangerous e.g. firearms, cannons, and small items that may be swallowed or ingested or may have latent defects all of which may cause harm to a person. Purchaser accepts all risk of loss or damage from its purchase of these items and Auctioneer disclaims any liability whether under contract or tort for damages and losses, direct or inconsequential, and expressly disclaims any warranty as to safety or usage of any lot sold.

**Dispute Resolution and Arbitration Provision:**

45. By placing a bid or otherwise participating in the auction, Bidder accepts these Terms and Conditions of Auction, and specifically agrees to the dispute resolution provided herein. Consumer disputes shall be resolved through court litigation which has an exclusive Dallas, Texas venue clause and jury waiver. Non-consumer dispute shall be determined in binding arbitration which arbitration replaces the right to go to court, including the right to a jury trial.
46. Auctioneer in no event shall be responsible for consequential damages, incidental damages, compensatory damages, or any other damages arising or claimed to be arising from the auction of any lot. In the event that Auctioneer cannot deliver the lot or subsequently it is established that the lot lacks title, or other transfer or condition issue is claimed, In such cases the sole remedy shall be limited to rescission of sale and refund of the amount paid by Bidder; in no case shall Auctioneer's maximum liability exceed the high bid on that lot, which bid shall be deemed for all purposes the value of the lot. After one year has elapsed, Auctioneer's maximum liability shall be limited to any commissions and fees Auctioneer earned on that lot.
47. In the event of an attribution error, Auctioneer may at its sole discretion, correct the error on the Internet, or, if discovered at a later date, to refund the buyer's purchase price without further obligation.
48. Dispute Resolution for Consumers and Non-Consumers: Any claim, dispute, or controversy in connection with, relating to and /or arising out of the Auction, participation in the Auction. Award of lots, damages of claims to lots, descriptions, condition reports, provenance, estimates, return and warranty rights, any interpretation of these Terms and Conditions, any alleged verbal modification of these Terms and Conditions and/or any purported settlement whether asserted in contract, tort, under Federal or State statute or regulation shall or any other matter: a) if presented by a consumer, be exclusively heard by, and the parties consent to, exclusive in personam jurisdiction in the State District Courts of Dallas County, Texas. THE PARTIES EXPRESSLY WAIVE ANY RIGHT TO TRIAL BY JURY. Any appeals shall be solely pursued in the appellate courts of the State of Texas; or b) for any claimant other than a consumer, the claim shall be presented in confidential binding arbitration before a single arbitrator, that the parties may agree upon, selected from the JAMS list of Texas arbitrators. The case is not to be administrated by JAMS; however, if the parties cannot agree on an arbitrator, then JAMS shall appoint the arbitrator and it shall be conducted under JAMS rules. The locale shall be Dallas Texas. The arbitrator's award may be enforced in any court of competent jurisdiction. Any party on any claim involving the purchase or sale of numismatic or related items may elect arbitration through binding PNG arbitration. Any claim must be brought within one (1) year of the alleged breach, default or misrepresentation or the claim is waived. This agreement and any claims shall be determined and construed under Texas law. The prevailing party (party that is awarded substantial and material relief on its claim or defense) may be awarded its reasonable attorneys' fees and costs.
49. No claims of any kind can be considered after the settlements have been made with the consignors. Any dispute after the settlement date is strictly between the Bidder and consignor without involvement or responsibility of the Auctioneer.
50. In consideration of their participation in or application for the Auction, a person or entity (whether the successful Bidder, a Bidder, a purchaser and/or other Auction participant or registrant) agrees that all disputes in any way relating to, arising under, connected with, or incidental to these Terms and Conditions and purchases, or default in payment thereof, shall be arbitrated pursuant to the arbitration provision. In the event that any matter including actions to compel arbitration, construe the agreement, actions in aid or arbitration or otherwise needs to be litigated, such litigation shall be exclusively in the Courts of the State of Texas, in Dallas County, Texas, and if necessary the corresponding appellate courts. For such actions, the successful Bidder, purchaser, or Auction participant also expressly submits himself to the personal jurisdiction of the State of Texas.
51. These Terms & Conditions provide specific remedies for occurrences in the auction and delivery process. Where such remedies are afforded, they shall be interpreted strictly. Bidder agrees that any claim shall utilize such remedies; Bidder making a claim in excess of those remedies provided in these Terms and Conditions agrees that in no case whatsoever shall Auctioneer's maximum liability exceed the high bid on that lot, which bid shall be deemed for all purposes the value of the lot.

**Miscellaneous:**

52. Agreements between Bidders and consignors to effectuate a non-sale of an item at Auction, inhibit bidding on a consigned item to enter into a private sale agreement for said item, or to utilize the Auctioneer's Auction to obtain sales for non-selling consigned items subsequent to the Auction, are strictly prohibited. If a subsequent sale of a previously consigned item occurs in violation of this provision, Auctioneer reserves the right to charge Bidder the applicable Buyer's Premium and consignor a Seller's Commission as determined for each auction venue and by the terms of the seller's agreement.
53. Acceptance of these Terms and Conditions qualifies Bidder as a client who has consented to be contacted by Heritage in the future. In conformity with "do-not-call" regulations promulgated by the Federal or State regulatory agencies, participation by the Bidder is affirmative consent to being contacted at the phone number shown in his application and this consent shall remain in effect until it is revoked in writing. Heritage may from time to time contact Bidder concerning sale, purchase, and auction opportunities available through Heritage and its affiliates and subsidiaries.
54. Rules of Construction: Auctioneer presents properties in a number of collectible fields, and as such, specific venues have promulgated supplemental Terms and Conditions. Nothing herein shall be construed to waive the general Terms and Conditions of Auction by these additional rules and shall be construed to give force and effect to the rules in their entirety.

**State Notices:**

Notice as to an Auction in California. Auctioneer has in compliance with Title 2.95 of the California Civil Code as amended October 11, 1993 Sec. 1812.600, posted with the California Secretary of State its bonds for it and its employees, and the auction is being conducted in compliance with Sec. 2338 of the Commercial Code and Sec. 535 of the Penal Code.

Notice as to an Auction in New York City. These Terms and Conditions are designed to conform to the applicable sections of the New York City Department of Consumer Affairs Rules and Regulations as Amended. This is a Public Auction Sale conducted by Auctioneer. The New York City licensed Auctioneers are Harvey Bennett, No. 0924050, and Samuel W. Foose, No.0952360, who will conduct the Auction on behalf of Heritage Auctions, Inc. ("Auctioneer"). All lots are subject to: the consignor's right to bid thereon in accord with these Terms and Conditions of Auction, consignor's option to receive advances on their consignments, and Auctioneer, in its sole discretion, may offer limited extended financing to registered bidders, in accord with Auctioneer's internal credit standards. A registered bidder may inquire whether a lot is subject to an advance or reserve. Auctioneer has made advances to various consignors in this sale.

Notice as to an Auction in Texas. In compliance with TDLR rule 67.100(c)(1), notice is hereby provided that this auction is covered by a Recovery Fund administered by the Texas Department of Licensing and Regulation, P.O. Box 12157, Austin, Texas 78711 (512) 463-6599. Any complaints may be directed to the same address.

Notice as to an Auction in Ohio: Auction firm and Auctioneer are licensed by the Dept. of Agriculture, and either the licensee is bonded in favor of the state or an aggrieved person may initiate a claim against the auction recovery fund created in Section 4707.25 of the Revised Code as a result of the licensee's actions, whichever is applicable.

Rev. 10-20-09

## Additional Terms & Conditions:
### COINS & CURRENCY

COINS and CURRENCY TERM A: Signature₀ Auctions are not on approval. No certified material may be returned because of possible differences of opinion with respect to the grade offered by any third-party organization, dealer, or service. No guarantee of grade is offered for uncertified Property sold and subsequently submitted to a third-party grading service. There are absolutely no exceptions to this policy. Under extremely limited circumstances, (e.g. gross cataloging error) a purchaser, who did not bid from the floor, may request Auctioneer to evaluate voiding a sale: such request must be made in writing detailing the alleged gross error; submission of the lot to the Auctioneer must be pre-approved by the Auctioneer; and bidder must notify Ron Brackemyre (1-800-8726467 Ext. 1312) in writing of such request within three (3) days of the non-floor bidder's receipt of the lot. Any lot that is to be evaluated must be in our offices within 30 days after Auction. Grading or method of manufacture do not qualify for this evaluation process nor do such complaints constitute a basis to challenge the authenticity of a lot. AFTER THAT 30-DAY PERIOD, NO LOTS MAY BE RETURNED FOR REASONS OTHER THAN AUTHENTICITY. Lots returned must be housed intact in their original holder. No lots purchased by floor Bidders may be returned (including those Bidders acting as agents for others) except for authenticity. Late remittance for purchases may be considered just cause to revoke all return privileges.

COINS and CURRENCY TERM B: Auctions conducted solely on the Internet THREE (3) DAY RETURN POLICY: Certified Coin and Uncertified and Certified Currency lots paid for within seven days of the Auction closing are sold with a three (3) day return privilege. You may return lots under the following conditions: Within three days of receipt of the lot, you must first notify Auctioneer by contacting Client Service by phone (1-800-872-6467) or e-mail (Bid@HA.com), and immediately ship the lot(s) fully insured to the attention of Returns, Heritage, 3500 Maple Avenue, 17th Floor, Dallas TX 75219-3941. Lots must be housed intact in their original holder and condition. You are responsible for the insured, safe delivery of any lots. A non-negotiable return fee of 5% of the purchase price ($10 per lot minimum) will be deducted from the refund for each returned lot or billed directly. Postage and handling fees are not refunded. After the three-day period (from receipt), no items may be returned for any reason. Late remittance for purchases revokes these Return privileges.

COINS and CURRENCY TERM C: Bidders who have inspected the lots prior to any Auction, or attended the Auction, or bid through an Agent, will not be granted any return privileges, except for reasons of authenticity.

COINS and CURRENCY TERM D: Coins sold referencing a third-party grading service are sold "as is" without any express or implied warranty, except for a guarantee by Auctioneer that they are genuine. Certain warranties may be available from the grading services and the Bidder is referred to them for further details: Numismatic Guaranty Corporation (NGC), P.O. Box 4776, Sarasota, FL 34230; Professional Coin Grading Service (PCGS), PO Box 9458, Newport Beach, CA 92658; ANACS, 6555 S. Kenton St. Ste. 303, Englewood, CO 80111; and Independent Coin Grading Co. (ICG), 7901 East Belleview Ave., Suite 50, Englewood, CO 80111.

COINS and CURRENCY TERM E: Notes sold referencing a third-party grading service are sold "as is" without any express or implied warranty, except for guarantee by Auctioneer that they are genuine. Grading, condition or other attributes of any lot may have a material effect on its value, and the opinion of others, including third-party grading services such as PCGS Currency, PMG, and CGA may differ with that of Auctioneer. Auctioneer shall not be bound by any prior or subsequent opinion, determination, or certification by any grading service. Bidder specifically waives any claim to right of return of any item because of the opinion, determination, or certification, or lack thereof, by any grading service. Certain warranties may be available from the grading services and the Bidder is referred to them for further details: Paper Money Guaranty (PMG), PO Box 4711, Sarasota FL 34230; PCGS Currency, PO Box 9458, Newport Beach, CA 92658; Currency Grading & Authentication (CGA), PO Box 418, Three Bridges, NJ 08887. Third party graded notes are not returnable for any reason whatsoever.

COINS and CURRENCY TERM F: Since we cannot examine encapsulated coins or notes, they are sold "as is" without our grading opinion, and may not be returned for any reason. Auctioneer shall not be liable for any patent or latent defect or controversy pertaining to or arising from any encapsulated collectible. In any such instance, purchaser's remedy, if any, shall be solely against the service certifying the collectible.

COINS and CURRENCY TERM G: Due to changing grading standards over time, differing interpretations, and to possible mishandling of items by subsequent owners, Auctioneer reserves the right to grade items differently than shown on certificates from any grading service that accompany the items. Auctioneer also reserves the right to grade items differently than the grades shown in the prior catalog should such items be reconsigned to any future auction.

COINS and CURRENCY TERM H: Although consensus grading is employed by most grading services, it should be noted as aforesaid that grading is not an exact science. In fact, it is entirely possible that if a lot is broken out of a plastic holder and resubmitted to another grading service or even to the same service, the lot could come back with a different grade assigned.

COINS and CURRENCY TERM I: Certification does not guarantee protection against the normal risks associated with potentially volatile markets. The degree of liquidity for certified coins and collectibles will vary according to general market conditions and the particular lot involved. For some lots there may be no active market at all at certain points in time.

COINS and CURRENCY TERM J: All non-certified coins and currency are guaranteed genuine, but are not guaranteed as to grade, since grading is a matter of opinion, an art and not a science, and therefore the opinion rendered by the Auctioneer or any third party grading service may not agree with the opinion of others (including trained experts), and the same expert may not grade the same item with the same grade at two different times. Auctioneer has graded the non-certified numismatic items, in the Auctioneer's opinion, to their current interpretation of the American Numismatic Association's standards as of the date the catalog was prepared. There is no guarantee or warranty implied or expressed that the grading standards utilized by the Auctioneer will meet the standards of any grading service at any time in the future.

COINS and CURRENCY TERM K: Storage of purchased coins and currency: Purchasers are advised that certain types of plastic may react with a coin's metal or transfer plasticizer to notes and may cause damage. Caution should be used to avoid storage in materials that are not inert.

COINS and CURRENCY TERM L: Storage of purchased coins and currency: Purchasers are advised that certain types of plastic may react with a coin's metal or transfer plasticizer to notes and may cause damage. Caution should be used to avoid storage in materials that are not inert.

COINS and CURRENCY TERM M: NOTE: Purchasers of rare coins or currency through Heritage have available the option of arbitration by the Professional Numismatists Guild (PNG); if an election is not made within ten (10) days of an unresolved dispute, Auctioneer may elect either PNG or A.A.A. Arbitration.

COINS and CURRENCY TERM N: For more information regarding Canadian lots attributed to the Charlton reference guides, please contact: Charlton International, PO Box 820, Station Willowdale B, North York, Ontario M2K 2R1 Canada.

WIRING INSTRUCTIONS:

BANK INFORMATION:
Wells Fargo Bank
420 Montgomery Street
San Francisco, CA 94104-1207

ACCOUNT NAME: Heritage Auction Galleries

ABA NUMBER: 121000248

ACCOUNT NUMBER: 4121930028

SWIFT CODE: WFBIUS6S

Rev. 7-24-09

# Your five most effective bidding techniques:

## ❶ Interactive Internet™ Proxy Bidding
(leave your maximum Bid at HA.com before the auction starts)

**Heritage's exclusive Interactive Internet™ system is fun and easy! Before you start, you must register online at HA.com and obtain your Username and Password.**

1. Login to the HA.com website, using your Username and Password.

2. Chose the specialty you're interested in at the top of the homepage (i.e. coins, currency, comics, movie posters, fine art, etc.).

3. Search or browse for the lots that interest you. Every auction has search features and a 'drop-down' menu list.

4. Select a lot by clicking on the link or the photo icon. Read the description, and view the full-color photography. Note that clicking on the image will enlarge the photo with amazing detail.

5. View the current opening bid. Below the lot description, note the historic pricing information to help you establish price levels. Clicking on a link will take you directly to our Permanent Auction Archives for more information and images.

6. If the current price is within your range, Bid! At the top of the lot page is a box containing the Current Bid and an entry box for your "Secret Maximum Bid" – the maximum amount you are willing to pay for the item before the Buyer's Premium is added. Click the button marked "Place Bid" (if you are not logged in, a login box will open first so you can enter your username (or e-mail address) and password.

7. After you are satisfied that all the information is correct, confirm your "Secret Maximum Bid" by clicking on the "Confirm Absentee Bid" button. You will receive immediate notification letting you know if you are now the top bidder, or if another bidder had previously bid higher than your amount. If you bid your maximum amount and someone has already bid higher, you will immediately know so you can concentrate on other lots.

8. Before the auction, if another bidder surpasses your "Secret Maximum Bid", you will be notified automatically by e-mail containing a link to review the lot and possibly bid higher.

9. Interactive Internet™ bidding closes at 10 P.M. Central Time the night before the session is offered in a floor event. Interactive Internet™ bidding closes two hours before live sessions where there is no floor bidding.

10. The Interactive Internet™ system generally opens the lot at the next increment above the second highest bid. As the high bidder, your "Secret Maximum Bid" will compete for you during the floor auction. Of course, it is possible in a Signature® or Grand Format live auction that you may be outbid on the floor or by a Heritage Live bidder after Internet bidding closes. Bid early, as the earliest bird wins in the event of a tie bid. For more information about bidding and bid increments, please see the section labeled "Bidding Options" found in the Terms & Conditions of this catalog.

11. After the auction, you will be notified of your success. It's that easy!

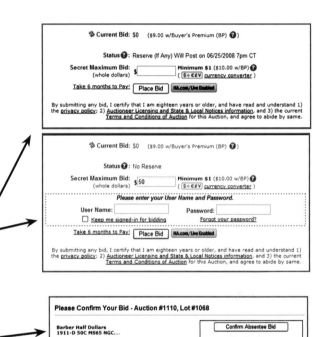

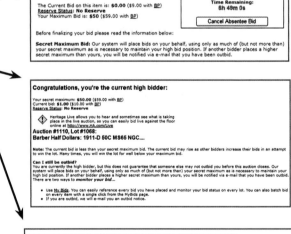

## ❷ HERITAGE Live!™ Bidding
**(participate in the Live auction via the Internet)**

1. Look on each auction's homepage to verify whether that auction is "HA.com/Live Enabled." All Signature® and Grand Format auctions use the HERITAGE Live!™ system, and many feature live audio and/or video. Determine your lots of interest and maximum bids.

2. Note on the auction's homepage the session dates and times (and especially time zones!) so you can plan your participation. You actually have two methods of using HERITAGE Live!™: a) you can leave a proxy bid through this system, much like the Interactive Internet™ (we recommend you do this before the session starts), or b) you can sit in front of your computer much as the audience is sitting in the auction room during the actual auction.

3. Login at HA.com/Live.

4. Until you become experienced (and this happens quickly!) you will want to login well before your lot comes up so you can watch the activity on other lots. It is as intuitive as participating in a live auction.

5. When your lot hits the auction block, you can continue to bid live against the floor and other live bidders by simply clicking the "Bid" button; the amount you are bidding is clearly displayed on the console.

## ❸ Mail Bidding
**(deposit your maximum Bid with the U.S.P.S. well before the auction starts)**

**Mail bidding at auction is fun and easy, but by eliminating the interactivity of our online systems, some of your bids may be outbid before you lick the stamp, and you will have no idea of your overall chances until the auction is over!**

1. Look through the printed catalog, and determine your lots of interest.

2. Research their market value by checking price lists and other price guidelines.

3. Fill out your bid sheet, entering your maximum bid on each lot. Bid using whole dollar amounts only. Verify your bids, because you are responsible for any errors you make! Please consult the Bidding Increments chart in the Terms & Conditions.

4. Please fill out your bid sheet completely! We also need: a) Your name and complete address for mailing invoices and lots; b) Your telephone number if any problems or changes arise; c) Your references; if you have not established credit with Heritage, you must send a 25% deposit, or list dealers with whom you have credit established; d) Total your bid sheet; add up all bids and list that total in the box; e) Sign your bid sheet, thereby agreeing to abide by the Terms & Conditions of Auction printed in the catalog.

5. Mail early, because preference is given to the first bid received in case of a tie.

6. When bidding by mail, you frequently purchase items at less than your maximum bid. Bidding generally opens at the next published increment above the second highest mail or Internet bid previously received; if additional floor, phone, or HERITAGE Live!™ bids are made, we act as your agent, bidding in increments over any additional bid until you win the lot or are outbid. For example, if you submitted a bid of $750, and the second highest bid was $375, bidding would start at $400; if no other bids were placed, you would purchase the lot for $400.

7. You can also Fax your Bid Sheet if time is short. Use our exclusive Fax Hotline: 214-443-8425.

## ❹ Telephone Bidding (when you are traveling, or do not have access to HERITAGE Live!™)

1. To participate in an auction by telephone, you must make preliminary arrangements with Client Services (Toll Free 866-835-3243) at least three days before the auction.

2. We strongly recommend that you place preliminary bids by mail or Internet if you intend to participate by telephone. On many occasions, this dual approach has reduced disappointments due to telephone (cell) problems, unexpected travel, late night sessions, and time zone differences. Keep a list of your preliminary bids, and we will help you avoid bidding against yourself.

## ❺ Attend in Person (whenever possible)

Auctions are fun, and we encourage you to attend as many as possible – although our HERITAGE Live!™ system brings all of the action right to your computer screen. Auction dates and session times are printed on the title page of each catalog, and appear on the homepage of each auction at HA.com. Join us if you can!

# Take 4 Months to Pay...

## Heritage will Finance Your Purchase

We're collectors too, and we understand that on occasion there is more to buy than there is cash. Consider Heritage's Extended Payment Plan [EPP] for your purchases totaling $2,500 or more.

### Extended Payment Plan [EPP] Conditions

- Minimum invoice total is $2,500.

- Minimum Down Payment is 25% of the total invoice.

- A signed and returned EPP Agreement is required.

- The EPP is subject to a 3% *fully refundable* Set-up Fee (based on the total invoice amount) payable as part of the first monthly payment.

- The 3% Set-up Fee is refundable provided all monthly payments are made by eCheck, bank draft, personal check drawn on good funds, or cash; and if all such payments are made according to the EPP schedule.

- Monthly payments can be automatically processed with an eCheck, Visa, or MasterCard.

- You may take up to four equal monthly payments to pay the balance.

- Interest is calculated at only 1% per month on the unpaid balance.

- Your EPP must be kept current or additional interest may apply.

- There is no penalty for paying off early.

- Shipment will be made when final payment is received.

- All traditional auction and sales policies still apply.

**There is no return privilege once you have confirmed your sale, and penalties can be incurred on cancelled invoices. To avoid additional fees, you must make your down payment within 14 days of the auction. All material purchased under the EPP will be physically secured by Heritage until paid in full.**

To exercise the EPP option, please notify **Eric Thomas** at **214.409.1241** or email at **EricT@HA.com** upon receipt of your invoice.

We appreciate your business and wish you good luck with your bidding.

# Heritage Auction Galleries
## Local Tax & International Shipping Information

CALIFORNIA - Local tax on purchases delivered at the auction:
If you wish to pick up your lots at or after the auction, you MUST present a valid resale certificate issued to you by the state of California. If you are registered as a dealer in your home country, you may obtain this for free from The Department of Revenue, 28 Civic Center Plaza #239, Santa Ana, CA 92712, Ph# 714 558 4059 or 800 400 7115.

NEW YORK - Local tax on purchases delivered at the auction:
If you wish to pick up your lots at or after the auction, you MUST present a valid resale certificate issued to you by the state of New York. If you are registered as a dealer in your home country, you may obtain this for free from The Department of Revenue, 55 Hansom Place, Brooklyn, NY 11217 - Ph# 718 722 2030.

This must be done before the auction, and sometimes takes months to complete. Please initiate this process early, and remember to renew your resale certificate every year. Bring your certificate or a good photocopy of it to the auction, so that we can copy the necessary numbers off of it. Heritage cannot grant exceptions to this, and we must collect [NY/CA] sales tax from you if you wish to pick up your lots at the sale without a valid resale certificate.

Shipping:
Heritage will ship items you have won to you if you wish. The buyer is responsible for shipping expenses AND insurance on the items sold. Heritage cannot insure items sent overseas by mail or by FedEx. Heritage CAN insure items sent by Air Freight, but this usually costs between $400 and $600, so please calculate if the amount of your purchase justifies this expense to you.

---

CALIFORNIA - Steuer auf Auktions kaeufe die am Auktionsort abgeholt werden:
Wenn Sie keine gültige Wiederverkaufbescheinigung haben, müssen wir Ihnen CA Steuer berrechnen. Um diese Steuer zu vermeiden, wenn Sie Ihre Ware waehrend oder nach der Auktion abholen, müssen Sie eine gültige Wiederverkaufbescheinigung überreichen, die Sie durch den Staat von [New York/Kalifornien] erhalten. Wenn Sie als ein Händler in Ihrem Heimatland registriert sind, können Sie dies umsonst erhalten The Department of Revenue, 28 Civic Center Plaza #239, Santa Ana, CA 92712, Ph# 714 558 4059 or 800 400 7115.

NEW YORK - Steuer auf Auktions kaeufe die am Auktionsort abgeholt werden:
Wenn Sie keine gültige Wiederverkaufbescheinigung haben, müssen wir Ihnen NY Steuer berrechnen. Um diese Steuer zu vermeiden, wenn Sie Ihre Ware waehrend oder nach der Auktion abholen, müssen Sie eine gültige Wiederverkaufbescheinigung überreichen, die Sie durch den Staat von New York erhalten. Wenn Sie als ein Händler in Ihrem Heimatland registriert sind, können Sie dies umsonst erhalten The Department of Revenue, 55 Hansom Place, Brooklyn, NY 11217 - Ph# 718 722 2030.

Dies muss vor der Auktion gemacht werden, und dauert manchmal Monate. Bitte leiten Sie dieses Verfahren früh ein und vergessen Sie nicht, Ihre Wiederverkaufbescheinigung jedes Jahr zu erneuern. Bringen Sie Ihre Bescheinigung (oder eine gute Photokopie davon) zur Auktion, dann können wir die notwendige Information davon kopieren. Heritage kann keine Ausnahmen zu dieser Vorschrift genehmigen.

Lieferung:
Wenn Sie wünschen, wird Heritage Ihnen Ihre ersteigerte Ware, liefern. Der Käufer ist verantwortlich für Portokosten UND Versicherung der Ware. Heritage kann Ware, die per Post oder FedEx nach Ubersee geschickt wird, nicht versichern. Heritage kann Ware versichern, die per Luftfracht geschickt wird, aber dies kostet gewöhnlich zwischen $400 und $600, deshalb kalkulieren Sie bitte, ob der Betrag Ihres Kaufes diese Ausgabe rechtfertigt.

---

CALIFORNIA - El impuesto local en compras entregadas en la subasta:
Si usted no tiene un certificado de reventa válido, tenemos que cabrar impuestos CA en sus compras. Para evitar los impuestos que pagan cuando usted recoge su gran cantidad en o después de la subasta, usted debe presentar un certificado de reventa válido publicado a usted por el estado de [Nueva York /California]. Si usted es registrado como un comerciante en su patria, usted puede obtener esto gratis en The Department of Revenue, 28 Civic Center Plaza #239, Santa Ana, CA 92712, Ph# 714 558 4059 or 800 400 7115.

NEW YORK - El impuesto local en compras entregadas en la subasta:
Si usted no tiene un certificado de reventa válido, tenemos que cabrar impuestos NY en sus compras. Para evitar los impuestos que pagan cuando usted recoge su gran cantidad en o después de la subasta, usted debe presentar un certificado de reventa válido publicado a usted por el estado de Nueva York. Si usted es registrado como un comerciante en su patria, usted puede obtener esto gratis en The Department of Revenue, 55 Hansom Place, Brooklyn, NY 11217 - Ph# 718 722 2030.

Esto debe ser hecho antes de la subasta, y toma a veces meses para completar. Inicie por favor este proceso temprano y recuerde de renovar su certificado de reventa todos los años. Traiga su certificado (o una fotocopia buena de el) a la subasta, de modo que podemos copiar los números necesarios de el. Heritage Auctions no puede hacer excepciones a esta política.

El envío:
Si usted desea, Heritage Auctions enviará los artículos que usted ha ganado. El comprador es responsable los gastos de enviar y el seguro en los artículos vendidos. Heritage Auctions no puede asegurar artículos mandados en el exterior por correo ni por FedEx. Heritage Auctions puede asegurar artículos mandados por flete aéreo, pero por esto cuesta generalmente entre $400 y $600, de modo que calcule por favor si la cantidad de su compra le justifica este gasto a usted.

---

CALIFORNIA - Tassa locale sugli acquisti consegnati all'asta:
Tutti gli acquisti effettuati all'asta e avuti in consegna all'asta stessa nella città di/nello stato di California sono soggetti alla tassa statale sulla vendita. La tassa sulla vendita non è applicabile solo se l'acquirente presenta un valido certificato di vendita al dettaglio emesso dallo stato / dalla città di The Department of Revenue, 28 Civic Center Plaza #239, Santa Ana, CA 92712, Ph# 714 558 4059 or 800 400 7115.

NEW YORK - Tassa locale sugli acquisti consegnati all'asta:
Tutti gli acquisti effettuati all'asta e avuti in consegna all'asta stessa nella città di/nello stato di New York sono soggetti alla tassa statale sulla vendita. La tassa sulla vendita non è applicabile solo se l'acquirente presenta un valido certificato di vendita al dettaglio emesso dallo stato / dalla città di The Department of Revenue, 55 Hansom Place, Brooklyn, NY 11217 - Ph# 718 722 2030.
A questa norma non vi sono eccezioni. Gli acquirenti possono presentare domanda per il certificato di vendita al dettaglio se hanno una partita VAT/IVA per la vendita al dettaglio del loro rispettivo Paese. I processo per la richiesta può durare mesi. Si prega quindi di programmarlo per tempo. Si ricordi che il certificato deve essere rinnovato ogni anno.

Spedizione:
Su richiesta, Heritage può spedire gli articoli acquistati all'asta. Spettano all'acquirente le spese di spedizione e l'assicurazione. Heritage non è in grado di assicurare gli articoli inviati all'estero attraverso la posta o FedEx. Heritage può solo assicurare gli articoli inviati per via aerea. La spesa può ammontare a 400-600 dollari USA o più, a seconda delle dimensioni degli articoli e del loro valore.

---

CALIFORNIA - Taxes locales et frais sur les achats récupérés après la vente aux enchères:
Si vous n'avez pas de certificat de revente valide, nous sommes dans l'obligation de vous réclamer la taxe à l'achat pour les Etats de Californie et New York. Pour éviter de payer ces frais quand vous récupérez vos lots à la vente ou après, vous êtes dans l'obligation de présenter un numéro de revente valide, issue par les Etats de Californie. Si vous êtes déjà enrégistré comme marchand dans votre pays, vous pouvez obtenir votre certificat gratuitement à l'adresse suivante The Department of Revenue, 28 Civic Center Plaza #239, Santa Ana, CA 92712, Ph# 714 558 4059 or 800 400 7115.

NEW YORK - Taxes locales et frais sur les achats récupérés après la vente aux enchères:
Si vous n'avez pas de certificat de revente valide, nous sommes dans l'obligation de vous réclamer la taxe à l'achat pour les Etats de New York. Pour éviter de payer ces frais quand vous récupérez vos lots à la vente ou après, vous êtes dans l'obligation de présenter un numéro de revente valide, issue par les Etats de New York. Si vous êtes déjà enrégistré comme marchand dans votre pays, vous pouvez obtenir votre certificat gratuitement à l'adresse suivante The Department of Revenue, 55 Hansom Place, Brooklyn, NY 11217 - Ph# 718 722 2030.

Cela doit être fait avant la vente aux enchères et prend souvent plusieurs mois de procédure. Veuillez commencer ce procédé suffisament tôt et renouveler votre certificat chaque année. Veuillez apporter votre certificat (ou une bonne photocopie) à la vente aux enchères afin que nous puissions enregistrer vos numéros de références. Héritage ne peut accorder d'exception à ce règlement.

Expédition:
Si vous le souhaitez, Héritage peut vous expédier les objets que vous avez obtenu. L'acquereur est responsable des frais de transports et d'assurances sur les lots achetés. Heritage ne couvre pas les frais d'assurances sur les objets envoyés à l'étranger par courier ou Fedex. Heritage peut seulement assurer les objets envoyés par Air Freight, mais à un tarif allant de $400 à $600. Veuillez vous assurer que le montant de vos achats justifie cette dépense.

---

Калифорния – местный налог на покупки с доставкой на аукционе:
Если вы хотите забрать приобретенные вами лоты во время или после аукциона, вы ДОЛЖНЫ предоставить действительный сертификат на перепродажу, выданный вам штатом Калифорния. Если вы зарегистрированы как дилер в своей стране, вы можете получить его бесплатно в налоговом отделе The Department of Revenue по адресу: 28 Civic Center Plaza #239, Santa Ana, CA 92712 или телефону: 714 558 4059 или 800 400 7115.

Нью-Йорк - местный налог на покупки с доставкой на аукционе:
Если вы хотите забрать приобретенные вами лоты во время или после аукциона, вы ДОЛЖНЫ предоставить действительный сертификат на перепродажу, выданный вам штатом Нью-Йорк. Если вы зарегистрированы как дилер в своей стране, вы можете получить его бесплатно в налоговом отделе The Department of Revenue по адресу: 55 Hansom Place, Brooklyn, NY 11217 или телефону: 718 722 2030.

Эти меры должны быть приняты до начала аукциона, и их осуществление может занять несколько месяцев. Пожалуйста, позаботьтесь об этом заранее и не забудьте также о ежегодном возобновлении сертификата на перепродажу. Имейте при себе подлинник сертификата или его фотокопию хорошего качества, что позволит нам сделать копии необходимых номеров. В данном случае «Наследие» не предоставляет исключений; в Калифорнии и Нью-Йорке мы обязаны взимать с вас налог на продажу в случаях, когда вы хотите забрать приобретенные вами лоты во время торгов без предоставления действительного сертификата на перепродажу.

Доставка
По вашему желанию «Наследие» обеспечит доставку приобретенных вами предметов. Покупатель несёт ответсвенность и за расходы по доставке, и за страховку на проданные предметы. «Наследие» не имеет возможности застраховать предметы, отправляемы за море через услуги почты или FedEx. «Наследие» ИМЕЕТ ВОЗМОЖНОСТЬ застраховать предметы, посылаемые воздушным фрахтом, что обычно сопряжено с дополнительными расходами от $400 до $600. Пожалуйста, примите в расчёт, насколько сумма вашего приобретения оправдывает такого рода затраты.

# LONG BEACH
## COIN, STAMP & COLLECTIBLES EXPO
Held at the Long Beach Convention Center

**FUTURE SHOW DATES**

### Official Auctioneer

The World's #1 Numismatic Auctioneer

**HERITAGE** HA.com
*Auction Galleries*

Feb 4-6, 2010
June 3-5, 2010
Sept 23-25, 2010

### Onsite Grading

PCGS
A Division of Collectors Universe
NASDAQ: CLCT

A Rare Commitment to Numismatics.
NGC
Numismatic Guaranty Corporation

Fun for the entire FAMILY! $$Multi-Million Dollar Exhibits$$! *Daily Gold Prize Drawings!*

## Santa Clara
## Coin, Stamp & Collectibles Expo
Held at the Santa Clara Convention Center

**FUTURE SHOW DATES**

November 19-22, 2009
April 8-11, 2010
November 18-21, 2010

Bring your Collectibles to our Expos for competitive offers from *America's Top Buyers!*

# www.exposunlimited.com

**FREE
Kids
Treasure Hunt**

EXPOS
UNLIMITED

**FREE
Educational
Seminars**

www.longbeachexpo.com

www.santaclaraexpo.com

**A Division of Collectors Universe, Inc. Nasdaq; CLCT
8 West Figueroa Street Santa Barbara, CA 93101
Ph (805)962-9939 Fx (805)963-0827
Email: warreckert@collectors.com**